MIRACLE IN
CANNIBAL COUNTRY
by Clarence W. Hall

Gift Publications
Costa Mesa, California 92626

Miracle in Cannibal Country

Copyright © 1980 by Gift Publications

Published by Gift Publications
Costa Mesa, California 92626

Library of Congress Catalog Card Number 80-67298
ISBN 0-86595-000-8

Bible references are taken from the King James Version.

CONTENTS

THE VOICE OF GOD

I

Sometimes God speaks in a still small voice,
Sometimes He speaks in the storm.
Sometimes we hear Him at evening time,
Sometimes in the early morn.
Sometimes He speaks in the midnight hour
When all is calm and still,
And if we listen to the voice of God
We're sure to know His will.

II

Sometimes God speaks when the going is rough
And we cannot see the way:
"Behold, I am with thee in this trial
And I always make the way.
For I know My own, and they hear My voice
And listen to what I say."
So when you hear the voice of God
Be still and know that it is He.
Obey whatever the Master says,
If pleasing you would be.
For those who obey the voice of God
By His Spirit are always led,
And their lives are pleasing unto Him
For they did whatever God said.

RUBY MASTERS

Received at the Fellowship
August 29, 1979

FOREWORD

A good question deserves a good answer.

And William Cameron Townsend, a young missionary to Guatemala in 1917, had no answer at all.

He had just removed a black, leatherbound Bible from his pouch and offered it to an ancient member of the Cakchiquel tribe. The wrinkled man had taken the book, flipped through a few pages, then blurted: "You say this is God's Word, senor, but it's written in Spanish, which few of my people know." Then he added: "If your God is so great, why can't He talk our Cakchiquel language?"

That blunt question helped change the direction of the young missionary's commitment. He vowed he would devote himself to giving God another tongue.

Going to live with the primitive Cakchiquels who, together with a dozen other tribes, constitute two-thirds of Guatemala's population, Townsend and his wife spent the next 12 years among them, serving their needs, eating their food, slowly mastering the difficult tongue and then reducing it to writing, something that had never been done before.

During that time, he accomplished more. He established five schools for the Cakchiquels, built a small hospital, acquired a printing press, produced a variety of literature in the native language—and, in the process, made hundreds of literate converts to Christianity. His proudest achievement: translating the entire New Testament into the Cakchiquel language.

Elated, Townsend thought: If this could be done for the Cakchiquels, why not for other illiterate tribes?

After all, Jesus had commanded: "Go ye into all the world and preach the gospel to every creature" (Mark 16:15).

Townsend began to wonder if putting the Bible into many native languages was supposed to be his part of Jesus' Great Commission.

Increasingly fascinated with the prospect of allying the science of linguistics to the spread of the Gospel, Townsend learned that in the world there were hundreds of separate and distinct language groups whose tongues had never been reduced to writing and who were therefore shut away from the Bible and the accumulated knowledge of the literate world.

For Townsend, to dream was to act. Leaving Guatemala, he set up a small summer course in an abandoned farmhouse in the Arkansas Ozarks, named it "Camp Wycliffe" for John Wycliffe, first translator of the Bible into English, and began with two dedicated students who had caught fire from his enthusiasm. These he taught all he had learned about the strange sounds and stranger grammar he had found among the Cakchiquels.

Camp Wycliffe's scant furnishings were nail kegs for sitting in classes, a big blackboard, and sleeping bunks padded with dry grass. The school's student body was slow in growth. There were only five students for the second summer, and 18 the third. But after two moves to better accommodations, and sending seven batches of trained translators to tribes in Mexico and Guatemala, there came a truly major move. The University of Oklahoma invited to its campus the "Summer Institute of Linguistics," as Camp Wycliffe was renamed, with college credit granted those who completed the eleven-week course.

Intrigued by the quality of linguistic training provided by Wycliffe's SIL, similar institutes were established at the Universities of North Dakota, Washington at Seattle, North Carolina at Charlotte, Texas at Arlington. Spreading abroad, SIL now includes nine linguistic institutes in six foreign countries.

Linguistic training was invaluable at the academic level. But, since Wycliffe's work was to be mainly with jungle tribes, more than academics was demanded. Hence, one of Townsend's first requirements of his translators was passage of a stiff course in the rigors of jungle living. He set up his first Jungle Training Camp in Mexico, and later established others in several strategic countries.

The gift of an airplane made possible another Townsend innovation: delivery of workers among tribes who could not otherwise be reached. Today, Wycliffe's Jungle Aviation and Radio Service (JAARS) operates a fleet of 55 aircraft—single-engine planes and helicopters to such short-take-off-landing (STOL) planes as the Helio Courier. JAARS operates an ingenious radio network which keeps in constant touch with jungle stations.

Today, the work that "Uncle Cam" Townsend established more than 40 years ago has become the largest of its kind in the world. The globe-girdling Wycliffe/SIL force—translators and linguists, anthropologists and construction workers, air pilots and radio technicians, plus physicians, nurses, teachers and all manner of other "support personnel"—now number more than 4000. Together they comprise the most courageous and highly dedicated group I have ever met. This is the suspenseful story of one of them. . . .

Clarence W. Hall

Chapter 1
NEW IN CANNIBAL COUNTRY

On a steaming day in 1969, deep in the wilds of the Sepik River valley of Papua New Guinea, a lone dugout canoe, powered by a sputtering outboard motor, pushed its uncertain way upriver. Aroused by the motor's noise, coveys of rare birds with rainbow plumage flitted through the jungle trees, huge river snakes slithered along the river banks, and crocodiles of fearsome length and girth rose languidly to the surface for a curious look at the invading craft, then sank back beneath the muddy waters.

This was New Guinea, second largest island in the world. Primordial and untamed, here was a land of green mystery and turbulent beauty. Least explored of any part of the inhabited world, it is the ancient home of an estimated three million people. A tribal society whose knowledge of the outside world was almost nil, its people had been kept apart for unknown centuries by 700 distinctly different languages. Few of these languages had ever been put into written form. Only a comparative few could speak or understand the polyglot tongue known as Pidgin (more correctly, Melanesian Pidgin) which served as a trade language, and these mostly along the coast.

And this was the fabled Sepik River, one of the world's great waterways, said by some to be more fearful than the Congo, less explored than the Amazon. To travel its 700-mile length is to journey back thousands of years, and to meet people living exactly as they have lived for untold eons.

Operating the boat was a seasoned Bible translator, Neal Kooyers, whose tribe location was also on the Sepik, but farther downriver. Seated in the dugout's stern, her hands gripping the sides of the tipsy craft to maintain balance, was Marilyn Laszlo, a pert and pretty young woman, her deep blue eyes darting from side to side of the river. She had reason to be excited, for now, after several false starts, she was closing in on a dream: to carry God's Word to some of the world's most remote people.

Marilyn, an effervescent farm girl from Valparaiso, Indiana, glanced ahead at Judy Rehburg, from Pittsburgh, Pennsylvania, seated in the dugout's midsection, wondering how her partner was reacting to this primitive country some 12,000 miles from home.

As the craft nosed between floating logs and drifting bog islands, Marilyn Laszlo's mind sped back over events that had delivered her into the rapidly growing ranks of Wycliffe Bible Translators.

To Marilyn's surprise, she had not been immediately dispatched to her chosen tribe. According to WBT practice, it was necessary for WBT newcomers to Papua New Guinea to stop for a while at Ukarumpa, the New Guinea base high in the mountains, to gain further training in linguistics and also to absorb the flavor and feel of this strange land. This rule applies whether the team is a married couple or, as in Marilyn's and Judy's case, a pair of single girls.

Another requisite for WBT's Papua New Guinea workers is that all translators and "support personnel" working with them must learn to speak and write Pidgin—the closest thing to a Papua New Guinea common language.

Still another rule—vitally important to WBT in teaming up workers—is that single girls in pairs must first live and work together for six months. Only thus, WBT believes, can it be discovered whether they are compatible for teaming in round-the-clock intimacy.

All that was now behind her, mused Marilyn. All the studies, the tests, the waiting. But what was ahead? She couldn't even guess. She thought of the life she'd left: scores of friends and close relatives who loved and admired her; the comfortable security of a teaching post at a nearby high school; an attractive air-conditioned apartment with push-button delights; a sleek new convertible; the band she played in; the church choir she sang in; the athletic events she participated in.

With all this tumbling through her mind, she whispered to herself: "What, in heaven's name, made me willing to trade all *that* for *this*?" And a divine voice from deep within her seemed to answer: "*I* did, Marilyn—and indeed in heaven's name. Remember?"

How could she forget? Her very first intimation that God wanted her for the mission field had come when, only nine years old, she was driving her father's tractor on the family farm outside Valparaiso. While the yen to be a missionary could not, at that age, be classified unmistakably as a definite "call," it was an impulse that came again and again, stayed with her throughout her youth, recurring with growing intensity whenever she listened with excitement to visiting missionaries at her home church (First Baptist, Valparaiso) telling their adventures for God in faraway places with strange-sounding names.

Now, half a world away from all she knew and loved, Marilyn was on her way to fulfilling her chosen mission: to live in the village of Hauna with the Sepik Iwam tribe, learn to speak their language, reduce it to written form, teach the people to read and write—then, her ultimate aim: to translate the Scriptures into the intricate Sepik Iwam language.

Some 500 miles from the mouth of the river, Marilyn was now traversing a section of the river not altogether unfamiliar to her. Weeks before, while seeking God's guidance in choosing her tribe, and awaiting her partner's arrival, she had gone on an exploratory trip upriver.

Given the opportunity to choose her place of service, she had asked only for "a pioneering post where no other Wycliffe worker had gone—or wants to go." When her advisors suggested that the Sepik Iwams would fit that description, she insisted on seeing for herself. They cautioned, "The Sepik people have a past history of head-hunting and general unpleasantness toward outsiders, and while the government has done a good job of putting down their violence and practice of sorcery, they've not been able to wipe these out entirely."

But since she was adamant, a view of the area and people was arranged. "You'll have to be flown from here at Ukarumpa to a place on the river called Ambunti, where there's an airstrip and a government post. At Ambunti you'll have to take a dugout canoe 110 miles upriver. May God go with you."

The twelve-hour trip upriver was a thriller. All along the Sepik, they chugged past villages built along the river banks, invariably stirring excitement among the villagers, some obviously seeing white women for the first time. Suddenly, after they rounded a river bend and turned off into a tributary, a large village lay before them. Like most of the settlements on the Sepik during floodtime (six months out of the year), the houses stood in water. But unlike other villages they had passed, this one had a hilly area of about three acres, a portion of land high and dry—and unoccupied. Excitedly,

Marilyn exclaimed: "This is it! They told me to look for a village with a mountain in its middle."

And it was Hauna. As they turned toward the shore, a fleet of canoes filled with black, naked natives swarmed out to meet them, chattering and gesticulating. Going ashore, the trio was surrounded by others of the tribe, all chattering excitedly.

Getting nowhere through the language barrier, Marilyn shouted above the uproar, *Upela save tok pisin?* ("Anybody here speak Pidgin English?") At this, one of the younger men in the crowd stepped forward. *Mipela tok pisin liklik,* he said ("I speak a little Pidgin"), explaining that he and a few others of the younger men had acquired the knowledge while working on a copra plantation on the coast.

Eventually, through volleying Pidgin back and forth, Marilyn was able to explain the reason for their presence. "We two women want to live a while in your village, learn your language and culture."

When this was relayed to the village leaders, a long, sober meeting was held, with the essence of the discussion passed along in Pidgin by the young men. After hours of palaver, a decision was finally reached when one of the subchiefs pointed out that these were white women, and therefore weaker specimens. He declared: "We are strong men, of a strong tribe. What harm could they do? Our enemies would laugh at us if we showed ourselves afraid of two women!"

That argument carried the day. After a vote was taken, the chief, an ancient tribesman of regal bearing, announced the decision: the white girls could come on a trial basis.

Elated, Marilyn and Judy thanked the tribesmen, promising to return soon to build themselves a house to live in.

But where could they build? The village was already crowded with 54 houses, all of them built on stilts to allow the seasonal high water to flow through. The small amount of land left had to be reserved for growth of the tribe.

Marilyn had an answer to that one. But when she pointed to the "mountain," the villagers quailed, explaining that their hilly section was actually an ancient cemetery, home of the dead, whose spirits would not take kindly to any invasion by mere mortals. Technically, it was pointed out, the mountain belonged to the ancient chief, who was not only the village's Mr. Big but also its chief witch doctor. As such, he knew from long experience the ruckus these spirits could raise.

But there was one fact: the spirits would bring no evil to the tribe, only to the young women. If they were willing to brave the spirits' wrath—well, it might be interesting to see what would happen.

Gravely the chief, Saperi by name, announced that the young white women could build a house for themselves on his "mountain."

Elated, they returned to Wycliffe's New Guinea base at Ukarumpa to gather their belongings and prepare themselves for the unknown of life in the tribe of the Sepik Iwams.

Chapter 2
ROUNDABOUT ROAD TO WYCLIFFE

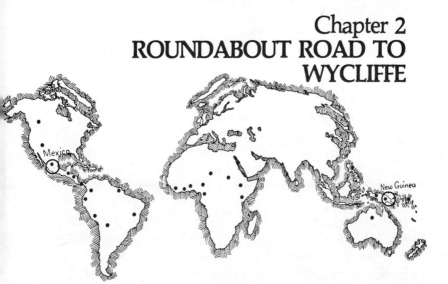

By what circuitous route was this Indiana farm girl led to link her life to Wycliffe Bible Translators, rather than to any one of many other mission groups actively recruiting workers? And how did it come about that, with 26 Wycliffe-occupied countries to choose from, she had wound up in Papua New Guinea when her original preferences lay elsewhere?

To find answers to these questions is to witness the workings of that divine imperative Christians refer to as "the call." Marilyn's story thus provides an illuminating example of the "hound of heaven" character of the Holy Spirit's pursuit.

During her high school days, after having a born-again experience at the age of 14, Marilyn poured most of her restless energy into sports—softball, basketball, volleyball and track on high school teams. She plunged also into music, studying voice, singing in the school glee club, playing trombone in the school band and plunking the strings of her guitar.

Described by classmates of both sexes as enormously popular, Marilyn nevertheless was no great scholar. And long discussions with a string of boyfriends and others as to what she was going to do with her life left her restive and uneasy. When she finished high school in 1951 (graduating seventh in a class of 12), her restlessness only increased. Vaguely suspecting that her dis-ease came from failure to surrender herself entirely to God's will for her life, she went through a period of uncertainty and agitation. Seeking to quiet her conscience, she shifted from job to job for four years: secretary, file clerk, doctor's office receptionist, work in a bearing factory and as a strawberry picker.

Finally taking her problem to her pastor, she was told with blunt kindness, "All this drifting is getting you nowhere, Marilyn. You know what your real calling is. Go to college, finish the course and prepare yourself for missionary duty."

It was just the push she needed. Choosing Bryan College, a small Christian liberal arts school in Dayton, Tennessee, she repeated her high school concentration on athletics, and was asked to teach physical education as well as to serve as coach to the girls' basketball team. In her junior year, Marilyn was elected "Homecoming Queen." Graduating from Bryan in 1959, she took a teaching position in her hometown, studying meanwhile at Indiana University for her master's degree in education, which she achieved in 1961.

Once again she allowed her call to missionary service to fade into the background. For five years she was deeply involved in teaching near her hometown of Valparaiso.

But one night she was jolted again by what she felt was a voice from heaven. "The Lord seemed to be saying to me, 'Marilyn, you promised when a very young girl that you would go to the mission field if I called you. I'm calling you now.'"

No longer trying to dodge the call, Marilyn nevertheless had to face a practical problem. She prayed, "Lord, You know that I've accumulated some debts. I can't leave these to my family. If You'll just give me time to pay off these debts, I promise not to welch any further on my promise to You."

In a matter of days, she lined up a history teaching post in

Marquette, Michigan. When she found that the salary was not enough to meet her debts, she moonlighted as a waitress, making hamburgers, working from five till midnight. She says, "Naturally, I got little sleep. How the Lord held me together, I'll never know. But He did." Result: She paid off all her debts in one year, with some money left over.

Marilyn knew that her next step was to settle upon what mission group she would work under. She knew little of mission boards, their needs or what they offered. So she reviewed a sheaf of brochures accumulated from various missionary groups, wrote them all for further information, and mailed the whole stack of letters at one time, praying, "Whichever one answers first, Lord, I'll take as Your choice for me."

The very first reply was from a mission she knew little about: the Wycliffe Bible Translators!

With the letter from Wycliffe came a batch of information describing the unique character of its worldwide mission. She was captivated by descriptions of the hundreds of primitive tribal groups whose languages had never been written, whose illiteracy shut them away from all world knowledge and civilizing influence—and, most important, from any chance to read God's Word for themselves.

Her interest caught fire when she learned Wycliffe's prime purpose: to send trained and dedicated workers to the most remote corners of the earth, to live among such tribespeople, learn their language, put it into written form, start them on the road to full literacy and new life—and eventually to translate the Scriptures for the tribes, "each in his own tongue."

Needed by Wycliffe, Marilyn read, were not only highly trained linguists but an equal number of "support workers" with all kinds of skills—everything from secretaries and printers to pilots and mechanics to keep WBT's fleet of planes flying and maintain its radio network.

She learned that WBT was tied to no single denomination, but cooperative with all. All workers were required to subscribe to basic evangelical beliefs, were expected to have a personal relationship with Christ, and to be wholly committed to His service. Beyond that, they should be graduates of a university or of a sound Bible institute.

All workers involved in any form of literacy and language learning were required to take an intensive course in descriptive linguistics at one of WBT's sponsored Summer Schools of Linguistics tied to a half dozen universities in the U.S. and abroad.

Following completion of the SIL course, taught by some of the world's top linguists, applicants to Wycliffe's ranks were put through three months of rugged "survival training" at its jungle training camp in Mexico—all to test their mettle and prove whether they could "take it."

Confident that God had, though in a curious way, pointed out His will for her, Marilyn filled in the formal application for Wycliffe membership. Eager to know if she would qualify, she was deterred not a whit by the fact that Wycliffe was a "faith mission," with every member, from the top administrators down to the latest recruit, expected to raise his own support, depending purely on faith. The WBT rule is firm: "Give full information without solicitation." Though some outsiders may consider this policy a hard one, WBT has proved over the years that it pays off in adding a deeper dimension to the meaning of faith.

Marilyn learned how effective is this principle of "no direct solicitation" when, just before she took off for the Summer

School of Linguistics at the University of Oklahoma, a dedicated couple pledged her a year's full financial support. Other friends and fellow church members have demonstrated an equal eagerness to act as home-partners in her work.

If she ever felt a fleeting worry over such total dependence on faith, Marilyn never showed it. As she puts it: "WBT is not for those with concern about 'security'—except as that security rests firmly on the biblical promise, 'My God shall supply all your needs.' There is no firmer security than that!"

Chapter 3
MEXICO OR NEW GUINEA?

James Chalmers

Just as Marilyn Laszlo had been led by God into the Wycliffe Bible Translators, so she was led, in an even more circuitous fashion, to choose New Guinea as her field of service. How this happened makes an interesting study in God's persistent way of working His will.

During her jungle survival course in Mexico, she had fallen in love with the country—and especially with tribal people she had contacted. Thus, when asked while at SIL to indicate her three top preferences, she had named Mexico first, "anywhere in South America" second, and Vietnam third. New Guinea did not figure at all. She had hardly arrived in Oklahoma, however, when she felt rather than heard God's voice saying, "Not Mexico, Marilyn, but New Guinea."

Making up that voice, it seemed, was a set of curious circumstances. For one thing, she found herself surrounded at SIL by applicants training for service in New Guinea, rather than those interested in Mexico. Such were her roommate, her companions at the dining table, her classmates. No matter how hard she tried to find a place in groups training for Mexico, she seemed herded, willy-nilly, into the company of those preparing for New Guinea. Furthermore, most of her SIL instructors were drawn from those with New Guinea service.

And there were other unplanned influences. Among them, the lives of such missionary greats as William Carey, George Grenfell, Adoniram Judson, David Livingstone. In the SIL library, Marilyn immersed herself in biographies of such missionary greats, reveling in their dedication and courage, measuring her own willingness to sacrifice by theirs.

Of all these towering figures, however, she found herself attracted most to James Chalmers, of the London Missionary Society, whose book, *Pioneering in New Guinea*, was everywhere regarded as a missionary classic. His intimate friend Robert Louis Stevenson had called Chalmers "the most attractive, simple, brave and interesting man in the whole Pacific." And though he had once confessed to "a great prejudice" against Christian missions, Stevenson later wrote Chalmers, "If only I had met you when I was a youth, how different my life would have been!"

In Chalmers' audacious courage, Marilyn felt a zesty challenge, and wept openly whenever she read and reread of that Easter morning in 1901 when, going up New Guinea's wild Fly River, Chalmers and a companion were attacked and beheaded, their flesh cut into pieces, cooked with sago and eaten on the same day.

Confused by the contrasting tugs between her long-time leanings toward Mexico and the feeling that the Holy Spirit was leading her toward New Guinea, Marilyn was plunged into deep depression.

To dispel that depression, she took a typically Marilyn-like step to solve the problem. One Friday morning, feeling that she "had to get off somewhere with the Lord, by myself" in order to come to terms with her dilemma, she loaded her laundry bag and headed for what she thought would be a quiet laundromat. But when she found the place overrun with chattering mothers and childish clamor, she swung her laundry bag over her shoulder and fled the raucous scene.

A few blocks farther on she came to Oklahoma University's sprawling football stadium, empty of all life in football's off-season. Even the adjoining tennis court was deserted. No place could be quieter or more conducive to sorting out troubled thoughts than an empty athletic field, she told herself. Inspecting the twelve-foot high fence topped with barbed wire, she noticed one of the tall gates standing narrowly ajar. On impulse she went through the gate, shut it and climbed to the very top bleacher. There she began a miserable, one-way talk with God. "Lord, You know I've given myself totally to You. I'll go where You want me to go. I feel drawn to Mexico, but all I hear from all sides since coming here is 'New Guinea, New Guinea.' Is this Your way of telling me to forget Mexico?"

No answer came. Finally, assailed by searing thirst and gnawing hunger, she gave up. Climbing down from the bleacher heights, she came to the gate she'd entered hours before. It was locked!

With mounting dismay she circled the stadium, trying every gate. All were securely padlocked. Hurrying back "up top," she could see students on their way to the dining hall. But all her shouting and waving were to no avail. The only person to come within her voice's range was a small boy on a bicycle. Hearing her call, he looked up, then pedaled rapidly away as though he had seen an apparition.

After hours of frantic efforts to attract attention, she finally accepted the idea that she would probably have to spend the night in the lonely stadium. So, before darkness settled, she arranged her laundry into a pillow, pulled a large bath towel over her, and lay down for another talk with God, pleading again for some divine direction that would allow her to work in

Mexico.

Finally falling asleep, she was awakened by a cloudburst. Drenched, she started down the cement stairs to find shelter beneath one of the ramps. But in her hurry to escape the rain, she tripped and fell, bounding down a dozen rows of steps, with her bag of laundry tumbling behind. The fall scraped a batch of skin from one knee, dripping blood. Limping across the field to a sheltered spot, she tripped over a water hose and fell into a puddle of water, adding a muddy mess to her blood-stained clothes.

Under the shelter, feeling beaten and exhausted, she again took up her monologue with God. "Lord," she prayed, "are You letting this happen to me to make me realize that Your plan for me is not Mexico, which I've so stubbornly wanted, but New Guinea? If so, Lord, I here and now yield!"

She nestled down on her sodden bag of laundry and fell into a deep and refreshing sleep—peaceful at last.

Bright and early the next morning, a pair of tennis players showed up at the adjoining courts and, startled, took in the gaunt but happy phantom that was Marilyn. A key to the stadium was quickly found, and she was delivered to her dorm.

Others might attribute her happenstance to all the succession of pressures she'd been through. But to Marilyn they all added up to a divine appointment and one that God would not allow her own wishes to thwart.

Her first act after getting back from her stadium experience was to make a new list of three preferences. All three were: "NEW GUINEA!"

From then on her deep depression vanished and her old ebullience returned in full force.

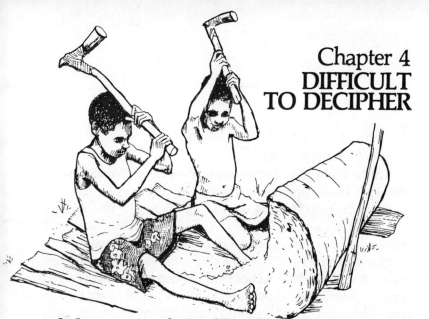

Chapter 4
DIFFICULT TO DECIPHER

In January 1969, the Wycliffe girls' arrival at Hauna in the mid-Sepik was greeted with something less than wild enthusiasm. True enough, some months before the tribe had agreed to their coming, and Chief Saperi had promised the use of his "mountain" for their house. But human minds are notably subject to change without notice. And soon it seemed obvious to Marilyn that it was only the Iwams' curiosity over the why of the white girls' presence that kept the reputedly warlike tribesmen from disposing of them according to their immemorial manner.

As for Marilyn and Judy, their initial plunge into primitive life and ways was not without its "culture shock." All their long and intensive training and anthropological study had not completely prepared them for the real thing. Here, home and civilization seemed far away. Here, the twentieth century dissolved like the morning mists off the Sepik.

But there was little time for worrying. A house of sorts had to be built on their allotted space. To help them get started, Wycliffe's base at Ukarumpa had sent up three support workers, trained in carpentry. During three weeks of back-breaking house construction, the girls were allowed to occupy an empty tribal house used by government agents on their occasional inspection visits.

Writing home, Marilyn described the 110-mile canoe trip up the Sepik from Ambunti to Hauna: "It took us two days (19 hours on the river) to get to our village. Traveling on the Sepik is not all mountains of fun. Crocodiles, mosquitoes and whirlpools can make it a questionable adventure. One unscheduled stop landed us on a sandbank, making it necessary for us to wade in three feet of mud to push ourselves back into deeper water. We didn't relish the idea of stepping on crocodiles. But such dangers and discomforts were soon forgotten in the joy of arriving at our village."

However, their joy faded a bit when, on their first night in the borrowed shack, they were assaulted by swarms of vicious mosquitoes, flying ants and other insects. Hastily rigging up mosquito nets, they crawled into bed and tried to forget their miseries by singing hymns to the accompaniment of Marilyn's guitar and the obligatos by the uninvited pests who came right through the nets. Meanwhile, king-sized cockroaches scampered across the floor and the tops of their nets. And over it all were the jungle night noises—cries of wild birds, grunts of crocodiles, sounds of night animals, insects and bats.

If the night brought nerve-testing sights and sounds, daylight replaced them with gentler manifestations, among them the laughter of little children who swarmed about, eager for further looks at the two women with the white skin. Since their house provided almost no privacy, Marilyn and Judy were constantly on display. Marilyn noted in her diary, "Each day brings what seems like a million bright and unblinking eyes to follow every move we make. It's like living in a glass house. But we are beginning to adjust to it all, and we thank the Lord for giving us so many wonderful little friends."

Making the rounds of Hauna early the next morning, Marilyn

observed that the village—one of five Sepik Iwam language groups in the area—consisted of 54 houses and approximately 400 people. Far from being a shiftless people such as outsiders imagined, sitting indolently beneath palm trees, these people, she rejoiced to find, were hard-working and industrious. The village throbbed with round-the-clock activity, its women pounding sago into paste, weaving baskets, keeping the children out of the way of the men spearing fish, felling trees for new homes, bringing in the sago palm, making dugout canoes, carving intricately designed shields. Everyone, including the children, had his appointed chores, and no one was allowed to shirk.

The tribespeople were endlessly fascinated by the girls' note-taking as they went about the village pointing to objects and asking their names, then writing them down phonetically. The pencil or pen they were using was called a *thorn*; the paper they wrote on was a *banana leaf*; the act of writing itself was *carving*. Most peculiar was the fact that in the Sepik Iwam language the center of life and seat of the emotions was the *throat*. Thus, in the tribal tongue one would never say, "I've asked Jesus to come into my heart." Instead he would say, "I've asked Jesus to come into my *throat*."

For all their handicaps in communication, Marilyn and Judy managed by gestures and smiles to win the tribe's trust. But they realized that before they could make any real headway, they had to become fluent in the language. Wycliffe's insistence on its workers learning the tribal language as a first step toward teaching literacy sets it apart from the approach made by some other linguists. Basic to this approach is the simple understanding that all peoples, no matter how primitive, possess great pride in their own language, and are immensely pleased when an outsider shows interest in learning and using it.

Says Marilyn, "The only language that will touch a tribe's heart is its mother tongue." Shortly, the two girls were proving the soundness of that theorem.

They quickly found that the Sepik Iwam language, like all of the other 700 tongues in New Guinea, was maddeningly difficult to decipher. It was this profusion of tongues that led James Chalmers, a century before, to declare that "this country must be the authentic site of the Tower of Babel!"

With such a language, it was easy, Marilyn found, to make embarrassing goofs. Once, addressing a tribal chief by name, she found she had lengthened the vowel sound so that she was calling him *louse*. Fortunately, the chief was not insulted, only amused.

Making the Sepik Iwam language so complex and difficult to master, Marilyn found, was its fantastic explicitness. To a tribesman, it is not enough to use a term denoting some particular action; there must be a word that describes the how and why and even the exact where of the action taken.

Take, for instance, the verb *to cut*. Cutting down a tree to build his house, the Sepik Iwam will use one word; if he's cutting it down for firewood, he will use another and very different one. The vocabulary goes on endlessly. Cutting bananas off the stalk, or whiskers off his face, or sago palm leaves for his roof—whatever the action or its reason, he uses words that sound like no other, no matter how close their context.

It took some six months to impart to the tribe what the white girls were really after. One day an elderly man, after watching Marilyn and Judy as they went about gathering words and writing them down, could restrain his curiosity no longer. Shyly, he came up to say, "Mama Marilyn, what are you carving on that banana leaf with that thorn?" Patiently,

Marilyn replied, "With this thorn we are carving your talk on this banana leaf so we can learn your talk and teach your people to carve it. Later we will give you God's talk on this banana leaf, just as He speaks it—and in your language."

Incredulous, the old man put out his hand, gently touched the paper, and said, "You mean to say, Mama Marilyn, that God's talk and our talk can be carved on the banana leaf for us to see and understand?" Assured that this was so, he turned away, hesitated a moment to shake his head, then said softly, "Marilyn, oh, Marilyn, why did it take you so long to come?"

That night she could not sleep. Echoing in her mind, the old man's words were unconsciously accusatory. Why, indeed, had Christian missions "taken so long" to get God's Word to these forgotten people? In the future when she would feel weary and down, she would remember those wistful words and freshly dedicate herself to whatever part of the world's spiritually hungry millions were to become her field of labor.

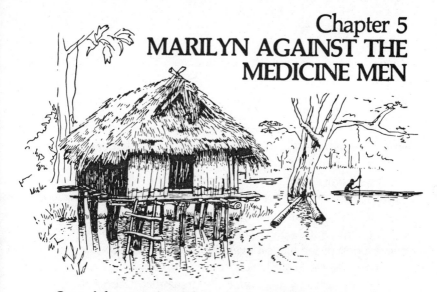

Chapter 5
MARILYN AGAINST THE MEDICINE MEN

One of the most fruitful contributors to the girls' acceptance by the tribe was the medical help they brought. As in most other New Guinea areas, the Sepik area was rife with diseases: malaria and tropical ulcers, elephantiasis and epilepsy, yaws and leprosy, respiratory and eye problems. Pneumonia was the number one killer, and life expectancy was about 35 years. With a large supply of modern miracle drugs, and careful training in dispensing them, Marilyn was soon performing what the Sepik Iwams felt were astounding acts of magic.

Previously, the only treatment for all physical ailments was by witch doctors. In Hauna alone there were 54 of these practitioners, some of them, like Chief Saperi, owner of the "mountain" containing Marilyn's house, the ruling heads of their clans. In the village milieu, all witch doctors who were not feared for their ability to summon evil spirits were highly respected. By no means were they all dealers in black magic or practitioners of jungle mumbo jumbo.

For the more common ailments, Marilyn found, the native medicine men had their own nostrums—some, surprisingly effective. They used secret herbs and practices unknown to civilized pharmacopeia, crude splints to heal broken bones, and tourniquets to stanch the flow of blood. They had a certain leaf that, when chewed, stopped pain; another, that treated diarrhea efficiently. Above all, they were skilled in primitive psychology to detect who was actually suffering and who was faking it.

Not so efficacious, however, were some of the "remedies" supplied by native doctors. One of the more curious "treatments" recommended to mothers for relieving pain of their babies and small children called for the capture and cooperation of the biggest available grasshopper. Locating what seemed to be the trouble source, the mother would gently rub the insect's scratchy legs over the area, then release it. If the grasshopper flew off, it was assumed that it was taking along the pain. If the insect showed no signs of trying to leave, it could be judged that the treatment was rejected.

But however strange such practices seemed to Marilyn, she never made the mistake of publicly putting down the native doctors or showing amusement at their antics. Instead, she sought to win their friendship, treating them as fellow healers, discussing modes of treatment and observing what techniques they had.

It was only when the native doctor went from medicine to forms of black magic that he and Marilyn parted company. At such times, spurred by superstitious relatives demanding a ritual ages old among New Guinea tribes, a witch doctor would take on a totally different personality. Going into fantastic gyrations and screaming in a high-pitched voice, he would call upon the evil spirit that allegedly caused the sickness. He would keep up this spine-tingling exercise for hours, even days, until he himself became "possessed"—at which time the evil spirit was supposedly exorcised. "In America," says Marilyn, "demon possession may be discounted by some, but out here it's a reality one can't deny."

Shortly after entering the tribe, Marilyn witnessed such a

performance—and luckily saved the day for both patient and the discredited witch doctor.

In this case, one of Marilyn's native language helpers named Ogmar became ill. When a villager rushed to Marilyn's house to call out, "Ogmar has big sick," she hurried to his house to find a witch doctor already at work. Marilyn watched quietly as the witch doctor went through his standard "treatment." Since the illness seemed seated in Ogmar's chest, the witch doctor had called for roots of a certain plant, supposedly the habitat of an avenging spirit. After going through a wild dance, he went into an elaborate act of chewing the root, then spitting the juice on the affected part of Ogmar's body. This charade went on for hours, but Ogmar's pain only grew worse.

Finally, the witch doctor slipped away into the darkness, whereupon Ogmar's relatives begged Marilyn, "Give him some of your shoot medicine, Mama Marilyn!" Loading her hypodermic needle, Marilyn gave Ogmar a shot with the "shiny thorn" and almost immediately the pain was gone. The people rejoiced but failed to understand why, with a pain in the chest or stomach, it was necessary to jab the patient in his buttocks with the "thorn."

From birth to death, the lives of the Sepik Iwams are governed by age-old health customs and conventions. For the pregnant woman, a whole list of taboos become operative. Among these are many confusing no-no's—all carrying penalties of varying degrees.

For example, the pregnant woman cannot eat fish that have fins or scales. If indulged in, the family witch doctor warns, her child's mouth will take the form of a fish, small and misshapen. Likewise *verboten* are bats, normally considered a dietary delicacy. To break this taboo is to risk the livelihood of the child having to grow up with buck teeth like those of the bat. A favorite fodder at any other time is swamp grass, a chewy substance similar to sugar cane. But for those undergoing pregnancy, its use will threaten lifelong chills for her child.

Prospective fathers also have their taboos. One of these decrees that if the father insists on building a canoe near birth time, his child's back or chest will be caved in like the canoe.

In the case of baby burial, the child is first covered with white mud as a sign of mourning. Shells containing a portion of mother's milk are placed on each side of the child's head so that its spirit will be sustained as it goes into the next world. Wrapped in bark, the little body is lowered into the grave. Sticks and leaves are carefully placed so that no dirt touches the body. In the case of an adult man, his canoe is chopped up and the pieces put on top of the leaves.

Another curious practice pertains to the bones of the dead, regarded to be of great value. After complete decomposition of the body, certain bones are disinterred and hung up in the deceased's house: the body's strongest—shoulder bones, thigh and arm bones—but always from the body's right side, never the left, which is the weakest. These bones supposedly keep the spirits of the dead from getting angry with the survivors and causing them harm.

With sickness so rife in the village, it was not long before the medical demands on Marilyn were making an outsized draft on her time and strength. Once convinced of the "shiny thorn's" curative powers, the villagers soon were clamoring for attention to their ills. Some even invented ailments to get it. Hence, Marilyn was soon treating as many as 75 patients a day.

When she found that caring for the sick was consuming time sorely needed for her language work, she recruited four of the village's brightest young men, trained them in spotting the signs of the more common diseases, in administering the required drugs and in applying bandages properly, and set up a small clinic. However, she stayed on call, day and night, to meet the needs of the more seriously stricken.

Going on sick calls in the middle of the night had its hazards. Typical was one black night in 1970 when the two girls were called from bed to attend a villager whose house was across the river. Marilyn aroused one of her helpers to ferry them across in a dugout canoe. In midriver the canoe hit a floating log, pitching her satchel of medicines, lantern and other supplies overboard. The canoe began filling with water. The helper, humiliated, paddled away, leaving Marilyn and Judy in shoulder-deep water to fend for themselves.

Hardest of all for Marilyn to bear was the desperate impotence of watching young children die because the people sometimes brought their sick to her when it was too late to save them.

And then there were the occasions when she was faced with situations beyond her competence. At such times, she had to call by radio for help from the doctor at Ukarumpa or Ambunti.

A villager was brought in with a big toe almost severed by a carelessly wielded machete. Serious infection had already set in. Nervously, Marilyn put in an emergency call to Ukarumpa and was told, "The toe will have to be cut off, Marilyn—and you'll have to do it. Time is of the essence."

Fighting off a wave of nausea, Marilyn objected, "But, Doctor, I know nothing of surgery. I've never cut off anything more serious than a hangnail."

"It's the only way," the doctor replied. "Get your sharpest knife, hone it down to a razor's edge. Sterilize the wound, then tell me when you're ready and do exactly what I tell you." Trembling, Marilyn followed the doctor's instruction to the letter, and in a matter of minutes the job was done. Within a few days, the wound was healed and the patient, minus a toe but alive and well, was fully recovered. "But," says Marilyn, "months had to pass before I could even look at a hot dog again without suffering a violent stomach turnover!"

Of her lifetime allergy to sickness—a real handicap in her situation—she says: "The last thing I ever wanted to be was a nurse. I can never go into a hospital to visit the sick without feeling sick myself. If anyone even suggests he or she is about to vomit, I beat them to it." Handicapped or not, she managed to minister to the sick in innovative ways.

Yet, with sickness so endemic and epidemics always threatening, Marilyn often felt she was fighting a losing battle. Convinced that many of the illnesses came from the polluted river water, she launched one of her most ambitious projects: the installation of four 2,000-gallon tanks to catch the rain water and pipe it to locations convenient to all villagers.

The only means of getting the huge tanks upriver to her village was by stages in four dugout canoes. This took several weeks. Once the tanks were installed, the people were persuaded to drink only fresh rain water, and pollution-caused illnesses declined.

Ordinarily possessed of an even, happy disposition, Marilyn was not always sugar-and-spice, as her tribe discovered. Though mostly held under control, her temper, when aroused, could scorch the atmosphere. The people got a taste of that temper when, during one of the disastrous pneumonia epidemics that periodically swept the village, a meeting of the tribe was called to bewail the dead and discuss methods of saving the sick. Standing off to one side, Marilyn listened in mounting anger as the elders finally agreed to leave it all up to the witch doctors.

Catching sight of Marilyn, the presiding chief called out: "Mama Marilyn, do you have any talk?"

"Do I!" she shot back. Straightening to her full five-feet-two, she strode to the center of the ring, blue eyes blazing. Hotly she said, "I wonder what I'm doing here. I came to Hauna as a friend—a friend who has not only strong medicine, as you know, but a strong Holy Spirit. In what you call my shiny thorn, I have medicine that, if used in time, could save many of your people from a burning death. But now you give me no chance to use this strong medicine. I may just as well pack up and go home!"

On and on she went, until one of her teachers stepped forward to say, "Marilyn is right. You are nothing but bush people!" Stung by this epithet, the crowd set up a chilling yell, surging toward the teacher with menacing clubs and canoe paddles.

In the middle of the melee, Marilyn, pushed and shoved from all sides, "felt that my time had come." But before she could be seriously harmed, another of her young teachers pulled her through the mob, got her into a canoe and paddled to safety across the river.

The village calmed down in a few days. Marilyn knew she had won the battle when, the next day, the people began bringing their sick to her house or asking her to come to theirs. By this time, she had no thought of leaving Hauna. Especially when one wizened little old woman, carrying a sick child in her arms, plaintively asked, "Now, Mama Marilyn, you won't 'pack up and go home?' Please, you stay?"

Tears starting, she hugged the bent old frame to her, drew a hand across the child's fevered brow, and said softly, "I stay."

Chapter 6
STRANGE CULTURE, STRANGER CUSTOMS

In no area of Marilyn's relationship with her tribe did she display more down-to-earth wisdom than in her behavior toward the Sepik Iwams' strange culture and customs. Strictly in line with Wycliffe policy, every translator is expected, during the first year with a tribe, to write an "anthropology paper" describing what was learned of the tribe's history, beliefs and superstitions, relationship with neighboring tribes, attitudes toward birth and death, marriage rules, their dress (if any), and food.

This study does not end with a translator's initial paper. It is revised, corrected and added to as new insights into tribal ways are gained. Over the years, therefore, a Wycliffe worker develops a large fund of scientific material of great value not only to Wycliffe workers themselves but also to outside ethnologists, anthropologists, archaeologists and other scholars.

From their very first day with the Sepik Iwams, Marilyn and Judy plunged into this learning process with vigor, carefully noting every action and reaction of the people, whom they observed in a lifestyle formed before history began.

Some of the age-old customs would have thrown less seasoned observers into culture shock: cannibalism and head-hunting, intertribal warfare and the practice of sorcery and black magic. Though such practices are slowly being brought under control by government patrol officers, they still exist to some degree in Sepik and such other remote areas as the New Guinea highlands.

Marilyn and her partner had scarcely settled in at Hauna village before she was reporting, "We had a case of both sorcery and cannibalism the other day. A young member of another language group downriver died suddenly, and relatives accused someone of causing his death by sorcery. Following an age-old custom of discovering the killer, the tribe dismembered the victim's body, then had every villager eat a piece of his flesh, cooked in a big pot. The theory was that whoever got sick and vomited was the guilty one. Unfortunately, no one got sick, so the mystery of the death is unsolved."

After witnessing a number of such cases, Marilyn concluded that "whatever one may believe about sorcery, it has been demonstrated that a New Guinean who believes that he has had sorcery worked against him will, in fact, sicken and quite often die for no apparent physical reason."

Warfare between tribes, and between clans within a tribe, is difficult to put down among a people long addicted to battle as the most effective way of settling differences.

Far more pervasive, however, and infinitely more difficult to combat is the spirit culture that rules Sepik Iwam lives from cradle to grave. Not only in this tribe but in virtually all of primitive New Guinea is society dominated by spirits—all of them reputedly evil. Not only is sickness always regarded as the work of some offended ancestral ghost, but death itself is never thought to be natural or inevitable; it is something caused by an avenging spirit or by some form of sorcery. The two often go together.

In this spirit-ridden world, the people's entire lives are given to placating the spirits. The Sepik Iwams, Marilyn discovered, had no gods as such, knew nothing of worship. Instead, they lived in dread of a whole pantheon of specters which inhabited the air, trees, rocks. To the Iwams, nothing otherworldly could be beneficent, only malicious, malevolent, sinister.

Thus, the fiction of the "happy savage," living an idyllic life, content in all his ways, possessing an inner peace unknown to more civilized cultures, is a romantic concept, but sadly out of focus. From the day he is born, the average primitive in Papua New Guinea lives with death—from the spears and arrows and stone-headed clubs of his enemies, from a variety of diseases, from sorcery in a hundred forms. Fears envelop his waking hours; he seldom knows a sense of security. The spirits of his ancestors are all about him, awaiting some pretext to do him in.

"What a joy it is for us," Marilyn confided to Judy one day, "to have the chance to show these people that we serve a God of love, a heavenly Spirit who wishes only good and not evil for all His children."

Thinking about their opportunity, the two girls felt a new surge of compassion for these, their adopted people—and a freshened commitment to their task of bringing God's Word to them in their own language.

Meanwhile, there were other bizarre customs that Marilyn found hard to take—especially burial alive of the very sick. One day she was told by a group from across the river that one of her best friends, named Neemau, had died. Leaping into her canoe, Marilyn paddled over to find a crowd wailing the death chant while a burial party was wrapping her friend in the usual burial bark and tying her body in vines.

Coming closer, Marilyn was shaken to find the woman obviously not dead, but in a coma. She cried out, "That's my good friend Neemau! She's not dead. Can't you see she is still breathing? You can't bury her! Let me take her to my house and revive her!" The head of the burial party paused only long enough to say, "Mama Marilyn, you don't understand. We shout in her ears, and she doesn't hear. Her eyes are open but she doesn't see. In that condition, she no longer lives. Her throat has died."

Forcibly restrained by the people from taking any other action, Marilyn later said, "On this occasion, I couldn't help feeling I'd witnessed a murder."

Throughout New Guinea, death due to any circumstance is celebrated with nonstop wailing, often for several days. Women relatives of the deceased smear their bodies and faces with clay, and neighbors helpfully join in their wailing. The men flail themselves with sharp leaves.

To demonstrate their grief, mothers and wives in other tribes whack off their own finger joints, then make a ritual of casting them into a bonfire lighted for the occasion. In at least one tribe, a widow avoids all adornment but the skull of her deceased husband, which is hung around her neck. Others use the skulls of dear ones for pillows.

The idea behind these gruesome practices is not so much to express grief as to forestall the anger of the departed's spirit.

More than those in any other Papua New Guinea area, the Sepik tribes are renowned for the number and artistic quality of their *tambarans* (spirit houses). Some tambarans are immense, up to four stories high and 200 feet long. Most are intricately carved and decorated with grotesque masks, figures, phallic symbols—and human skulls. All tambarans are strictly off limits to women. In some, skulls of ancestors crowd the interior, with tribesmen using them as pillows.

Scarcely less macabre are ceremonies initiating boys into manhood. These usually start with frenzied tribal dancing (to frighten the women away), then are followed with the ceremonial incisions cut into the boy's back. The purpose of the mysterious ceremony is to test the boy for fortitude—how to bear pain, and to instruct him in tribal lore, discipline and endurance. He is then run through a gauntlet to be flogged from all sides with thorned branches. Then comes the ceremony of boring the nose septum with a sharpened bone. If he goes through these tests, the boy is given a new name, declared a man, and permitted to strut proudly before the tribe—especially through the female element.

Girls in Papua New Guinea have it easier—at first. Until marriage, usually in her early teens, a "young fella meri" lives a comparatively carefree life, does little work, adorns herself with as many shells and feathers as her family can afford, and awaits the best bid for marriage. But marriage changes all that. She then becomes a drudge, tending gardens, toting firewood, pounding out and cooking sago, making bilium nets and baskets.

Courtship and marriage customs are complicated, with almost all the signals being called by the village elders. When a boy takes more than casual interest in a girl, the parents of both go into action. The parents of the boy make the first move, fanning out into the jungle to gather a quantity of the grass from which the tribespeople weave their sleep mats. This material is then ceremoniously taken over to the girl's house and loud inquiry is directed to her parents: Will their daughter, who is lucky enough to have found favor in their son's sight, make a nice sleeping mat for him?

A long argument ensues, during which each set of parents recites a long list of their offspring's virtues. If during all this hubbub the girl touches the material, the engagement is on. If she refuses and walks haughtily away, the deal is off. And neither set of parents will try to force the matter.

Almost universal throughout Papua New Guinea is the practice of "bride price." Brides don't come cheap. The going rate for a young girl in good health may run as high as the equivalent of $500 in pigs, shells, axes and spears. Hence, many brides are chosen when mere children, bought on the installment plan. A boy's family makes a downpayment to reserve the girl, then makes other payments as she develops.

If a girl thus bought remains puny, her value falls. If she gives promise of becoming a fat, strong wife who can bear many children and work well in the fields, her price shoots up. If she wants to back out before marriage, she can—with, of course, the return of the bride price and much interfamily haggling.

But once married, she usually stays that way—unless stolen by a rival tribe. "Woman stealing" is not uncommon, and is the cause of many quarrels, and even wars. Polygamy is freely practiced among those who can afford it—and is not objected to by a first wife, who can thus transfer some of her own drudgery onto the newcomer.

In Marilyn's view, not all native customs are evil or need replacement. On the plus side, for example, are the Sepik Iwams' strong family structure, their loyalty to their clans, their deep love and concern for their children, their tribal cohesion, their industry and intelligence. Elders are treated with respect and deference. In their society, every member has his assigned tasks and chores, from the youngest to the eldest.

Of these plus factors in the Sepik Iwam lifestyle, Marilyn speaks warmly: "We missionaries make a serious mistake if, when we move into a culture different from our own, we judge that everything needs to be changed. I refuse to utter condemnation of any practice, however baleful it may seem at first, until I understand why it developed."

For example, take the matter of native nudity—which, she says, seems to be more of a hang-up for the folks at home than for missionaries on the field. "Before coming to Papua New Guinea," she admits, "I wondered how long it would take to get used to naked natives all around me. Actually, it took about 24 hours. Today, if we supply our people with clothing from the States, it has nothing to do with modesty—only with protecting them from the hot sun, swarming insects and thorns, or giving them warmth on chilly nights."

One of Marilyn's favorites is her story of an old man who, coming every day to help her with language learning, was given a pair of belted trousers as pay. Previously, his only dress was a vine around his waist. Delighted, the old man got in his canoe and paddled back to his clan. When he returned the next day, proud as a peacock, he was still bedecked. But the trousers he carried over his arm. All he wore was the belt!

Among other features of Sepik Iwam life that cause at least mild culture shock in some newcomers is the tribe's cuisine. Though Marilyn learned to take some native diet items without gagging, there were others that incited rebellion in her innards. And in spite of her eagerness not to offend her people, who insisted that eating their food was the only way to make learning of their language easier, there were some items she couldn't keep down.

Shortly after settling in at Hauna, she was brought what they considered a great delicacy: a stick full of roasted grubs, a Sepik-style shish kebab. Proudly they extended their gift, then stood back to watch her enjoy it. Marilyn took one look at the item and uttered a devout prayer: "Lord Jesus, I don't want to offend these beautiful people. I'm willing to eat this all up if You're willing to keep it all down!" Her prayer was answered, for when put to the test, popping the grubs into her mouth, "my queasy stomach accepted the token!"

Easier to take, she found, was the tribe's staple—sago, obtained from the pithy stem of the sago palms that grow wild in the jungle, and pounded into a mushy compound. Other delicacies she tried to avoid eating were crisply fried flying ants, large, fat caterpillars and field mice.

For the most part, Marilyn and her various imported helpers lived off foods brought in from Australia: canned goods, yams, dried vegetables and fruits, and occasional treats of wild boar and ducks hunted by the tribesmen. Fish, of course, were plentiful, though they tended to be wormy.

Nevertheless, there were times when, due to delays of shipments upriver, their larder was so low that they had to make do with whatever native dishes they could stomach. At such times Marilyn was heard to mutter, "What I wouldn't give for a nice, juicy hamburger and a chocolate sundae with nuts and cherries on top!"

Chapter 7
BERLITZ ON THE SEPIK

Joel

Danny

When after long months, Marilyn and her partner felt able to communicate adequately in the tribal tongue, they knew they were ready to teach the people to read and write in their own language. In many respects this was the hardest and most time-consuming part of their total task, which Marilyn had divided into four phases:

    1) Make friends with the people, create trust, absorb as much of the tribal culture as possible;

    2) Learn to understand and speak the tribal tongue;

    3) Make the people literate in their own language;

    4) Translate the Scriptures into the Sepik Iwam tongue.

After two years in the tribe, Marilyn and Judy had accomplished the first two objectives. Phase two had been difficult enough. It had been spent in intensive language learning and analysis, assembling a dictionary of words and terms, deciphering the meaning of sounds, searching out patterns of grammatical structure. Now it was time to tackle phase three.

The method to be used to make the tribe literate was a modification of that developed by "Uncle Cam," Wycliffe's founder. Of it he had reported, "The Lord has given me a new system to teach reading. I call it the 'psycho-phonetic' method.

The alphabet is phonemic—each letter standing for only one sound. And instead of throwing the whole alphabet at the learners at once, I form words with just four or five letters. That way they can be reading a few words the first day. This gives them confidence. Each day I add a few more letters, and make words using all that they have learned to that point. Adults can learn to read in a month or less."

The magic in the Townsend method shortly proved itself, and soon tribal youngsters were racing through the village to proclaim their new knowledge.

Lacking any other facility for a classroom, or any other spot not flooded six months out of the year, the first school met in the space beneath Marilyn's stilt house. This make-do arrangement had to be followed until 1974, when Marilyn talked the tribal leaders into a building program that featured construction of the largest structure ever built on the "mountain": a schoolhouse 90 feet long and 24 feet wide, containing 10 classrooms and a large assembly room. The schoolhouse took 200 tribesmen three months to build, with the builders dragging in huge logs faster than the carpenters could cut them down. Also going up during 1974 were four other buildings: a clinic, a store, a church and a translation house. The very size and scope of this building program imparted a sense of permanency, a feeling among the tribespeople that literacy, along with the boons it brought, had come to stay.

Teachers were chosen from the brightest of the tribe's young men, most of whom had been helpful to Marilyn and Judy as they learned the Sepik Iwam language.

Before opening the school to the whole village, the appointed teachers themselves had to prove they were thoroughly grounded in the art of reading and writing their own language. After six months of speeded-up study and tests, Marilyn felt they were ready.

Appointed principal of the infant school was twenty-year-old Dani Adiyawai, youngest son of Chief Saperi. Another of the girls' language helpers, Joel Yapawi by name, was made assistant school principal, later to become pastor of the village church that, in time, came to be built. Both young men had become dedicated Christians.

These teachers, plus 18 others of like enthusiasm and ability, were not appointed by Marilyn but were chosen, at her insistence, by the tribal chiefs. The usefulness of all 20 was enhanced by their having been "outside" to work at coffee plantations nearer the coast, and having picked up a working knowledge of Pidgin.

Marilyn was convinced that, if their literacy program were to succeed, the whole village, young and old, had to be involved, including some of the influential tribal elders. She finally won cooperation of the elders by making them a sort of advisory council for the school, dubbing them "the Big Men," and saying it was up to them to see that the ancient culture of the tribe was properly protected and preserved. Proud of this attention, they took their assignment with enthusiasm.

During every stage of the school's development, Marilyn was careful to seek their counsel, patiently explaining over and over again what she was trying to do. On the Big Men she pinned the responsibility of setting standards and dealing with disciplinary problems. For instance, when one teacher began showing more than academic interest in some of the girl students, the council promptly hauled him before the village and suspended him for two months.

Other oldsters were also invited to attend school, but not many came at first, fearing ridicule for sitting with youngsters who could more quickly grasp the new teaching. To help close the forming generation gap, Marilyn enlisted the young to snare the old. In one clan, a young boy badgered his grandfather for days, begging him to go with him to school. The old man resisted, saying, "My head is too hard. The young can learn strange new ways, but not the old."

But finally the old man gave in. At school, when he found he could pick out a few words, the old man's joy knew no bounds. And the youngster, composing a little song of praise, went proudly singing through the tribe, "Grandfather is going to school: His hair is grey, his back is bent. He is very, very old. But Grandfather is going to school!"

The little school began slowly, due to the villagers' uncertainty as to what it was all about. But it picked up steam as students spread the word and gleefully displayed their ability to "handle the thorn and carve our talk on the banana leaf."

Teaching aids were minimal at first, consisting only of a homemade blackboard, erasers and a few pieces of chalk. Later, the students made their own slates and rough benches.

As attendance grew to 30, Marilyn, a firm believer in small teaching classes, split up the student body into groups of five each. Shortly, these groups were spread out all over the "mountain."

In the beginning, however, tribal interest in learning to read and write their own language was neither constant nor rapid. New and imaginative incentives had to be applied. The people had to be shown that literacy possessed material as well as spiritual advantages.

After a few months, interest in reading waned, and Marilyn was troubled. While attending a translators' workshop at the Ukarumpa base, she lay sleepless one night, trying to find a solution for her problem.

Then an idea popped into her superactive mind, again

demonstrating her talent for recharging motivation.

As Marilyn tells it, "When leaving Hauna for periods, I had made a practice of asking the people for a list of items they'd like me to buy for them and bring back. On this occasion, their list ran to such things as shovels, axes, hammers, fishing hooks and lines.

"Thinking over my shopping list, I decided to write the people a letter, informing them of additional items I'd found available at Ukarumpa. In my letter I asked, 'Do you want me to get these too?' If so, they could let me know their wishes via letter."

Then, making a number of copies of the letter, she talked the pilot of a plane, due to fly over Hauna in a few days, into dropping the letters. When these showered down, the people ran about in excitement, gathering up the copies. But no one was available to read them.

When Marilyn returned to Hauna, she asked, "Did you get the letter I sent you by plane?" The crestfallen villagers replied, "Yes, Mama Marilyn, but how could we know what you had carved on the banana leaf? We can't read our talk!"

Marilyn, with a straight face, told them what items she'd found available at Ukarumpa and could have gotten for them, adding, "What a pity you can't read your language. Think of the things you might have had!"

Attendance at school promptly soared.

Another powerful incentive to learning was added when Marilyn began the production of little books. With the aid of occasional short-term workers from Ukarumpa, plus a duplicator someone had sent her, she began to turn out simple primers for each student. Carrying the primers about with them became a badge of erudition.

Even sharper motivation to learn was stimulated when

Marilyn formed what she called "Writers' Workshops." In these, students were assigned to write, in their own language, stories descriptive of their most exciting experiences, observations on their native culture, and tribal legends. Not only did her students, young and old, find these exercises engaging; Marilyn herself found them revelatory of the tribe's interests, their ways of looking at life, and their anthropology.

Reporting to her home church in Valparaiso on the outstanding success of the Writers' Workshops, Marilyn said, "In one month we produced more than 1,000 pages of material for these books, and have typed up about 500 pages and had them printed. Each story carries the byline of the author—and are they proud of that! They love to see their names in the book, and there's keen competition to see who can produce the best story."

Except for the primers, the books were not given away but sold for a small charge. The amount paid was not beyond even the poorest of the tribe. But Marilyn is adamant on the principle that "we only really appreciate those things for which we work or pay." From the funds received she began to assemble a large and varied library.

In addition to such "working books" as the five basic primers used in class—the completion of which enables a student to read and write the Sepik Iwam language fluently—Marilyn's students have turned out signed stories of tribal folklore garnered largely from the old men's memories; accounts of adventures in hunting and fishing; books on tropical diseases and how to avoid and treat them; and many other how-to books on building canoes and houses, hand-carving and other arts and crafts for which Sepik peoples are noted, and even hymnbooks and tribal songs made up of their own compositions.

There are few things, insists Marilyn, tnat have done more to keep interest in literacy high and constant than her Writers' Workshops. Some of these little books are written in both the tribal language and in Pidgin.

Chapter 8
OH, FOR THE RIGHT WORDS!

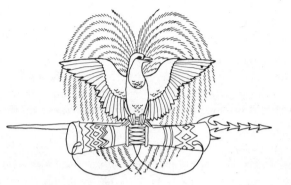

In 1974, with internal self-government slated for Papua New Guinea in September 1975, and with full independence promised for 1977, Marilyn redoubled her efforts to bring to her adopted people a sense of nationhood and citizenship responsibility. Among tribes so geographically remote from the center of the government, this took some doing. But workshops in what nationhood really means slowly brought the people around to seeing themselves as part of something big and important.

One means of imparting this was through teaching the Pidgin language. There being no immediate hope of turning any one of the new country's 700 tongues into an acceptable national *lingua franca*, Pidgin, used by nearly a million New Guineans, would have to serve.

Along with classes in reading and writing in Sepik Iwam, Marilyn established classes in Pidgin, making even her more primitive tribespeople truly bilingual.

Compared with most tribal tongues, Pidgin is relatively easy to learn, once one grasps a few basic words and gets the hang of its colorful but convoluted syntax. For instance, take such words as *kisim* for carry or bring, *kaikai* for food of any kind, *susu* for milk, *bokis* for box, *meri* for any female, *nogut* for bad or no good, *dispela* for this. If you ask for a glass of milk, you'll say in Pidgin, *Kisim susu bilong bullmakau meri.* Or if you've overeaten, you'll probably confess that *mi kaikai planti tumas.* If you're using a crosscut saw, you'd probably describe it as *pulim i kam, pusim i go.* Or noting a balding pate, you might comment, *het bilong em i nogat planti gras.*

If your canoe has a motor attached, you'll pronounce the latter as *ensin,* the canoe paddle as *pul bilong kanu.* Any little thing you see along the way is *liklik samting.* Pointing to a firefly, your Pidgin speaker is likely to describe it as *liklik binating* (little insect) *i gat sutlam long baksait bilong en,* which is self-descriptive. Or, if you're snapping a native's picture, you would say, *Yu lukluk stret long mi plis.*

Terms with religious connotation are likewise expressive and colorful. A church is *haus lotu* (worship house). The Bible is *book tambu.* Heaven is *ples antap.* The assurance of God's care and protection is expressed as *God i sambai yu.* Whereas to do something wrong is pointed out in the phrase, *mekim samting nogut.*

To take communion is *kisim Komunio,* whereas to break the Ten Commandments is *brukim ol mandato.* A worker of sorcery is described in Pidgin as *man bilong mekim posin.*

The Psalms: *singsing bilong David.* A prophet's warning: *toktok bilong saveman.* The Devil: *ensel* (angel) *nogut.* Heaven: *ples antap* (place on top). The Sabbath: *de bilong God.* A disciple: *boi bilong Jisas.* The incarnation: *Son bilong God i kamap man.*

One of Marilyn's major frustrations was not being able to find a term for the word *forgiveness.* She made up her mind to keep trying and praying.

Chapter 9
MOTIVATION BY MARILYN

It is doubtful that there is any Christian mission anywhere in the world where the people are more deeply involved in their own uplift than are the people of Hauna. Visit this remote section of the Sepik at any season or any time of day, and your first impression is that of a humming beehive of activity. Working happily at any one of a dozen tasks related to Bible translation or a host of other self-improvement tasks are busy people in every age bracket—young children to aged men and women.

Such a whirl of activity is not accidental. Nor is it due to any native love of industry. It is almost entirely due, as any of them will tell you, to the inspiration imparted to them by the spirit of the tireless young woman who has turned Hauna into the magical place it is.

Watching Marilyn Laszlo in action (and you'll seldom see her any other way), you will probably be reminded of Nehemiah, the prophet who recruited all elements of society to rebuild the tumbled Jerusalem walls. Explanatory of the success of that piece of work is simply the fact that "the people had a mind to work."

If there is one word that sums up Marilyn's success, it is "involve." From the start in Hauna, she made it plain that whatever was to be accomplished would have to come from the involvement of everyone. She never shaded down that principle. Constantly she kept before her people the fact that if a new day was to dawn over the Sepik, the people—all the people—would have to supply the necessary faith and work. Having motivated them to want something, she next had to involve them in ways to get it.

Thus she recruited the old men who, challenged to preserve the old culture, were appointed the "Big Men" and helped in rounding up the brightest of the young men to teach the young to read and write their own language and, later, to help translate the Bible.

Flattered at being consulted, the Big Men, who, at first, were cold to Marilyn's presence and program, sat solemnly to audit the teaching and pass upon how well the teachers had taught and the young had learned.

And, later, when Marilyn set up her Writers' Workshops to supply books for all classes, the Big Men proudly regaled the embryo writers with stories and legends out of the tribe's history. Immensely impressed by the attention being given to tribal culture (which the elders had long felt was somehow slipping away), the Big Men developed new dignity and a heightened interest in Marilyn's program.

As with the winning over of the old men, Marilyn applied the same kind of motivation and involvement to all the age groups, not only keeping them busy but imparting ethnic pride in preserving the tribe's past.

Another measure of Marilyn's success has been the almost total lack of young people who have left Hauna for greener pastures. Unlike other developing societies which lose a large proportion of their ablest young men after they have gained an education of sorts, Hauna's loss has been strikingly small. The explanation can only be that life in Hauna, with all that has been going on, has been infinitely more exciting and challenging than any other place.

"Motivate the people to want something better out of life," Marilyn was given to saying, "then involve them in ways to get what they want, and you'll soon see them on their way up."

Chapter 10
TOWERING TASK—BIBLE TRANSLATION

By 1974, having brought many tribespeople through the process of learning to read and write their own language, Marilyn Laszlo felt ready to concentrate on the intricate task of translating the Scriptures.

This was the goal toward which all her labor had been aimed. Important as was the achievement of literacy in a tribe whose language had never been written, the bringing of the Word was by far the most important. It was to this that she had devoted her life.

Preparing for her task, Marilyn felt alternately excited and overwhelmed. The excitement lasted; the sense of being overwhelmed faded. Describing her feelings at the time, she said, "I've learned to take it all to God—and He reminds me, 'This is not your job, Marilyn. You lead the life and present the Gospel, and leave the rest to Me.'"

With typical thoroughness, Marilyn prepared for the delicate and intricate process of Bible translation. Choosing her 10 brightest and most advanced schoolteachers, she put them through three months' training, then divided them into five teams.

Since the first objective was the four Gospels and the Book of Acts of the Apostles, each of the teams was assigned a separate book. Lacking any other Bible translation, a Pidgin New Testament had to serve as the general source book. For her own reference, Marilyn had a small library of several of the translations available in English, plus a shelf of such works as a Greek lexicon, a concordance and a Bible dictionary.

Drilled constantly into the Bible translation teams was the difference between this work and that used in the schools. "Remember always," she would say, "that the words in this Book are not schoolbook words, or man's words. They are God's. As you try to translate them, look for *meanings*. And, above all, pray that God's Holy Spirit will make their meanings clear to you."

Besides her 10 helpers, Marilyn appointed two other literacy teachers to serve as "back translators." Marilyn herself moved from team to team, helping to clarify a passage, referring to her library, looking always for meanings and how to express them. At regular intervals she would take the young translators with her to Ukarumpa, where expert consultants passed upon their work, pointing out errors, encouraging with praise when it was deserved.

Most stimulating of all, however, was Marilyn's own excitement over the whole process. One day of each week she would call together all those involved. From each translator's work of that week a passage would be chosen, put on the blackboard and discussed. Lively debates would ensue, with each saying what the passage meant to him, and how its meaning could be best expressed in the tribal language.

In line with Marilyn's commitment to involve the whole tribe in her total program, all villagers were invited to sit in on "God's talk." Especially invited were the "Big Men." They seldom missed one of the evening sessions, arguing between themselves far into the night over what new thing God had told the translators.

By such means, Marilyn kept interest in Scripture translation high throughout the village. Not that finding an exact word or passage was easy. Some almost defied literal translation, and there were some words of theological connotation for which the tribal tongue had no one-word equivalent. For example: faith, love, sin, redemption, repentance, forgiveness.

Translation from one tongue to another can be sticky, especially when the idioms of one language are not known to another. Says Dr. Kenneth L. Pike, president emeritus of Wycliffe's Summer Institute of Linguistics, "Some words give special difficulty. For instance, how does one translate the word *desert* to a jungle people who have never known anything like a desert? And how does one choose a word for *love* if the tribal words available vary in meaning from *pity* to *friendship* to *being sweet on somebody?*"

But there were other words and expressions whose meaning could be more easily translated. Thus, God's heartbreak over man's sin as expressed in John 3:16 became "God so hurt in His throat that He gave His only Son as 'payback for man's wrongdoing.'" To glorify God, the native translators agreed, really meant to "brag about God." There being no native words for Holy Spirit, the translators finally agreed on "the perfect, good Spirit."

And there were other examples of renditions using the people's idioms. The counsel of Christ to "Take no thought for the morrow" became *Do not worry about what is to come next day.* A hypocrite was described as *a person with two throats.* And the Great Commission to "Go ye into all the world" became, simply, *Upstream, downstream, everywhere go!"*

Christ's description of Himself as the Bread of Life was greeted with shudders. The Sepik Iwam people's only taste of bread had been a sample of a loaf from Marilyn. Their stomachs' reaction to this strange food was to throw up. If "bread" was allowed to stand, therefore, it would mean to them that belief in Christ was *that which makes us sick.* The simple change from "bread" to *sago* (the tribe's staple food) quickly solved that problem.

When the work of Marilyn and her staff had gotten their portion of the Word as clear as they could make it, the job was still a long way from being completed. They had to make many trips back and forth to Ukarumpa, Wycliffe's regional base, where teams of expert linguist-anthropologists and Bible scholars put their work through the most meticulous examination.

Within three years (by 1977) Marilyn and her staff had produced, in rough form, the translation of the four Gospels and the Book of Acts, or about two-thirds of the New Testament. "It will have to be done over and over, of course," she admitted, "for it must be as perfect and clear as human minds, guided by His mind, can make it."

There is no record that Marilyn ever lost even a tiny fraction of the excitement she felt in translating God's Word. She wrote home, "Sometimes the job seems overwhelming, and you wonder where you get the temerity to take on so huge a task. But how rewarding it is to see lives being changed as these beautiful people grasp its meaning and power!"

Working at their task from early morning till late at night was a mental and physical drain on Marilyn and the translation staff. So Marilyn found it necessary to arrange for occasional breaks in the routine.

Following a particularly long and intensive session of Bible translating, Marilyn rewarded 10 of her more accomplished native translators with a week's trip to Wewak, busy center on Papua New Guinea's north coast. Here they stayed for an eye-opening week, frolicking for the first time in salt water, staring in wonder at the big ships coming in and out of the port, gawking at the signs of business enterprise, asking questions galore about the white man's ways.

Though three of the 10 had visited Wewak briefly years before, none had ever before stayed at a hotel or eaten in a restaurant. Baffled at the array of silverware and dishes, but determined not to show themselves off as country bumpkins, they carefully kept a surreptitious eye on how Marilyn handled the profusion of knives and forks and followed her lead. At breakfast, served with such strange eatables as coffee and ham and eggs, one whispered to his tablemates, "Marilyn has paid for all this; we must eat it all!" They did, with manly grace.

Most memorable to all were their visits to business and government figures. Speaking in Pidgin, businessmen graciously took time to explain Papua trade, and government officials took time to tell them about their country, how it was governed and their hopes for its future. On their part, the 10, speaking in Pidgin, told their Wewak hosts proudly about their village, its school, its government and the strides it was taking toward building a better life for all. Commented one businessman, "I find these young men exactly the kind it will take to build our new country well!"

The days spent at Wewak were a time of discovery for all, including Marilyn herself.

Chapter 11
THE JOSEPH AFFAIR

Joseph

The years leading up to 1974, when Marilyn's work underwent wide expansion, were not all times of immediate triumph. During her early period with the tribe, it often seemed to her that troubles of various kinds, masterminded by Satan himself, were in league to sap her physical and spiritual reserves. That she was able to come through them all without cracking up is testimony to her dauntless courage.

Typically, Marilyn pinned all credit for her spiritual durability on the prayers and support of her backers at home. Time after time, after describing some deep trial, she would add, "I could feel—really *feel*—your prayers holding me up. How I love you for that!"

Marilyn's testing came in both large and small doses. Chief among the latter were the unending battles with nature. Housekeeping chores on the Sepik are chores indeed. In a climate where everything quickly molds, erodes and tarnishes, hours have to be spent just to keep tape recorders, cameras, lanterns and primus stoves in working condition. Vital parts rusted and had to be replaced. Clothing and bedding mildewed overnight, smelling moldy. Ants, roaches and termites ate her books and papers. Rats and mice built homes in her house, scampering through the rafters at night. Spiders flung their webs everywhere and had to be swept away every morning.

Yet Marilyn managed, fuming only over the "large chunks of God's time" that it took to wage war on such destroyers. Once she was heard to mutter that "Solomon knew what he was talking about when he declared that it's the little foxes that spoil the vines!"

But there were bigger foxes to be dealt with. Most ravaging of these in the beginning was the stinging opposition from a small but bitter clique led by Joseph, brilliant but unstable elder son of Chief Saperi. Sizing him up as a born leader, she saw in Joseph a man who could be of invaluable help to her program.

Fluent in Pidgin and quick of mind, he easily grasped the importance of his people becoming literate, and willingly sat for hours helping the two white girls with the tribal language. Further making him a force to be reckoned with was his appointed position as the official government representative in the village. For months he served in the dual job as teacher in the school and as keeper of the little store set up by Marilyn to supply items needed to produce village income, mainly from canoe-building and selling crocodile skins.

Then, suddenly, something in Joseph's character slipped. First sign of the slippage was the disappearance of small items and sums of money from the store. Joseph was found to be the culprit. Each time he feigned repentance, and each time Marilyn gave him another chance.

However, his next offense was more serious. After the death of his wife in a flu epidemic, Joseph became a Don Juan. His liaison with a single girl for whom the "bride price" had been paid by another was whispered throughout the village. Aware of the condemnation his action aroused, he hastily married the girl. But they had been married only three months when the girl gave birth to a baby.

Now Marilyn knew she had to face Joseph with more than mild reproof. The whole village was waiting to see what response, if any, she would make. Their reaction could go either way, favoring her stand or condemning her. The incident, she knew, put her whole program in jeopardy.

Calling the pair to her house, she pulled no punches. "Joseph," she said, "you know you have shamed yourself and this girl before the whole village. By this time you know that Christians do not do such things."

Guiltily, Joseph flew into a rage. He was innocent of any wrong, he declared. But how about the baby? Joseph fumed, "The baby was a miracle!" Marilyn replied, "Not a miracle, Joseph, but a sin. And since God cannot honor any work with sin in the camp, I cannot allow you to continue in the school."

At that, Joseph's fury rose to that of a madman. Shouting imprecations and threats, he declared, "You are on my clan's land. I'll burn down your school and your house and you in it!"

Thoroughly shaken, Marilyn managed to keep calm. "I've given you several chances, Joseph, and you've failed me every time. But God doesn't give up on the wrongdoers, and I won't either."

During the ensuing months, she kept her promise, lying awake nights trying to find ways to involve him again in her program without condoning his sin. Every day she prayed, "Lord, I've done everything I know how to do with this fellow, and I can't handle him. You must do something with him, Lord, please, he's Yours!"

Joseph's acrimony toward Marilyn reached its hottest point one day when he was called to a council of government representatives in Ambunti charged with reporting on village affairs. He angrily told of fanciful "upsets" at Hauna—pinning the blame on Marilyn's mission and demanding that her school

62   *Miracle in Cannibal Country*

be closed down.

The council of government representatives promptly issued an order to close the school until an investigation could be made. When news of the order reached Hauna, Marilyn and seven of her teachers headed downriver for Ambunti. Arriving before the meeting broke up, school principal Dani and the others demanded a hearing.

As spokesman, Dani, Chief Saperi's youngest son, said hotly, "Our village and its school are shamed by the lies spoken against us by my brother." He went into details of Joseph's fabrications, then said, "If you gentlemen wish, we will bring our whole tribe here to testify to what a happy state our fine school has brought us."

At this, the chairman banged his gavel and declared, "The former order is hereby rescinded. Meeting dismissed."

It took almost two years for Joseph to come to himself. But just before Marilyn was due to go home on furlough she prayed for and God suggested a way to bring him around. She had just acquired a new motor for her dugout canoe—and Joseph loved motors. Calling him in, she said, "Joseph, I want to put you in charge of the motors. My friends back in America have given me a new 25 horsepower motor. This one we'll reserve solely for your use and that of your clan. In return, you'll supervise the building of a new house for me. Mine is falling into ruin. We'll make a contract to that effect. Is it a deal?"

Overjoyed, Joseph wrote up the contract and both solemnly signed it. From that day on, there was no serious trouble with the former troublemaker. And after a period of trial, he was restored to the program and became one of Marilyn's top translators—and one of her staunchest friends.

A second cross the irrepressible Marilyn had to bear, especially during early years in the tribe, were recurrent illnesses. The body that had been built into prime condition by youthful athletics fell victim again and again to a bewildering assortment of diseases. Responsible for most of such ailments as pneumonia, malaria and the flu were the miasmic climate of the Sepik, constant exposure to the tribe's illnesses, and the frequent village epidemics.

But not the least of the causes was the driving schedule to which she subjected herself. Concerned with the health of her adopted people, Marilyn flagrantly neglected her own. Never one to pace herself, she plunged into her work as though there were no tomorrow. When stricken by some illness, she worried only over the time lost. On one occasion, after reporting off-handedly that she had been laid low by some ailment, she wrote home, "Now I've got to move at a faster pace to catch up!"

It took some doing to make her see that at least some of her ills might have been brought on by her excessive drive to "get the job done." If she wrote back-home supporters at all about any of her bouts with ill health, she was more likely to ask for prayer to stand the delay it caused than to pray for healing.

Marilyn was confident she knew who and what was behind her physical troubles. While recuperating from one of her many illnesses, she fell from a hammock onto a small wooden stool, breaking several ribs. Laid up for several days, she was told, "Maybe God, in allowing these things to happen, is trying to tell you something." She replied, "No, this is Satan's work. Haven't you noticed that every time we start translating the Word, something happens to bring the work to a halt?"

At the height of these troubles, Marilyn lost her pioneer partner of six years, Judy Rehburg, who moved on to work with another tribe. From then on, with trained translators at a premium, Marilyn had to make do with a series of volunteer short-term helpers sent out from Ukarumpa. While all these were, without exception, fine, dedicated girls, none could stay long enough to learn the language and get into the involved business of literacy and Bible translation. And even if they could stay, they could never catch up with Marilyn's head start. The only answer seemed to be to train her own translation partners, chosen from her staff of young men teachers who had shown themselves so adept at learning to read, write and teach their own language.

While undergoing these trials, Marilyn was fortunate in finding at Ukarumpa a devoted friend to help her through her darkest hours—Beverly Entz, wife of an aviation specialist at the base. "I never saw Marilyn shrink from what to others seemed an unsolvable predicament," says Beverly. "On dozens of occasions I've seen her attack such problems, grimly muttering, 'I'm not sure I can do this, but I'll lick it or die trying.'"

Probably the closest she ever came to that grim alternative was when, during an overlong stay in Hauna without relief or relaxation, she pushed herself close to total collapse. Sensing that something was seriously awry in her physical condition, she left for the States. She was sent first to White Springs Memorial Hospital at Lancaster, South Carolina, then to Billings Hospital in Chicago. The diagnosis at both places revealed the trouble: a severe case of trichinosis. To her physicians' surprise, further probing revealed that she had had—and somehow recovered from—a whole string of such other maladies as infectious hepatitis, hypoglycemia and mononucleosis, plus what one doctor called "a whole body full of malaria." She was told, "You have no business being alive, young woman. All our findings indicate that you should have succumbed long ago!"

Recovering slowly, Marilyn was in the States for 18 months,

the longest time she had ever been away from her village. But even while still hospitalized, she continued to be "my countrified self." Calling for her ever-present guitar, she sang and played for the nurses, made her room a mecca for ambulatory patients, spreading cheer everywhere with a lively "singalong."

Finally gaining outpatient status, she devoted her recovery time to deputation work in nearby churches and among her growing group of supporters.

A third major encumbrance to Marilyn's restless drive to get things done during her early years at Hauna was the necessity of depending upon river transportation. Demanded were constant back-and-forth trips to Ambunti for supplies, as well as for checking and double-checking every step of her Bible work with Wycliffe's expert consultants at its big base at Ukarumpa. While the second leg of this trip (Ambunti to Ukarumpa) was by Wycliffe's planes, the first and roughest leg (110 miles) had to be by dugout canoe.

True enough, though she had acquired a couple of outboard motors to power her dugout canoes, the motors had the bad habit of breaking down when needed the most. And neither she nor her helpers had the needed skills to keep them in good repair. When her motors conked out, often at the same time, there was nothing for her helpers to do but drift down the 110 miles to Ambunti, where Wycliffe maintained mechanics.

Among the mechanics, Marilyn became the butt of good-natured jibes at her mechanical incompetence. Seeing her coming, they would set up the cry, "Run for the jungle, fellows! Here comes Marilyn!" On one occasion when one saw her trying to change a spark plug, he was heard to sigh, "Next time, Marilyn, why not just say a prayer and leave the repairs to us!"

But the stress and strain of total dependence upon river travel was not very amusing. At one time she nearly lost her life when a large double canoe crashed into hers, ripping off the whole bow of her canoe and filling the craft with water.

Though when she first planned to settle in Hauna village, Marilyn had expected helicopter service to her village, almost nine years passed before such service was available. Yet, despite the additional burden the lack of suitable transportation placed upon her, there is no record of her ever complaining. Serenely she insisted, "When God wants us to have a helicopter, He'll see that we get it."

From Headquarters in Huntington Beach, California, Wycliffe Bible Translators conducts its world-wide ministry of translating the Bible into hundreds of languages.

Two leaders meet at Wycliffe Bible Translators' Jungle Aviation and Radio Service (JAARS) in Waxhaw, North Carolina: Demos Shakarian (left) founder/president of the Full Gospel Business Men's Fellowship International, and William Cameron Townsend (Uncle Cam), founder of Wycliffe Bible Translators.

Hauna Village on the Sepik River as Marilyn Laszlo and her companion first saw the land of the Sepik Iwam tribe.

Trees cut down to be made into canoes are moved to clearings.

(Above) Every tribesman has his canoe—even the very young. During high water time, it's his only way to get around.

(Above) One of Marilyn's most ambitious projects was this all-purpose community center. Seventy feet long and two stories high, it provided room for Bible translation teams, a school, a clinic and store.

To reduce illness from water pollution, Marilyn took on the tedious task of having tanks ferried in by canoe for the purpose of catching rain water.

Not all of the tribe's 54 medicine men were quacks. The better ones, such as this man, observed Marilyn's medical techniques and asked questions.

Before natives could be given a Bible in their own language, they had to learn to read. Three years before becoming a teacher, this man shown was illiterate.

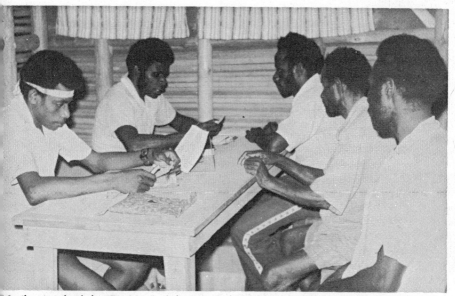

Marilyn involved the "Big Men" of the tribe in her Bible project by having them read and rule upon the clarity of the New Testament translating done by the younger men.

Ministering to the bodily ills of the people was a sure-fire friend-maker for Marilyn. Here she patches up a bruised shin.

Among the dozen young scholar-teachers was Dani, youngest son of Chief Saperi, who later became principal of the school.

A touch of Marilyn's home state, Indiana, is shown by the Hoosier T-shirt of one of the Sepik Iwam students who not only learned to read and write but also how to teach others.

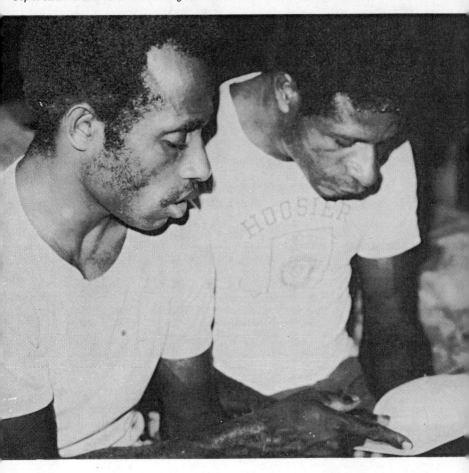

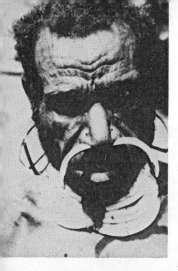

Chief Saperi, tribal ruler and head witch doctor, became Marilyn's staunchest backer for her Bible translation project.

(Below) This teacher named Paul helped educate his people so they could eventually learn to read the Bible in their native tongue.

ce the Sepik Iwams mastered their own language, Marilyn started a writer's workshop, t of which came a steady flow of stories about their own experiences and tribal history.

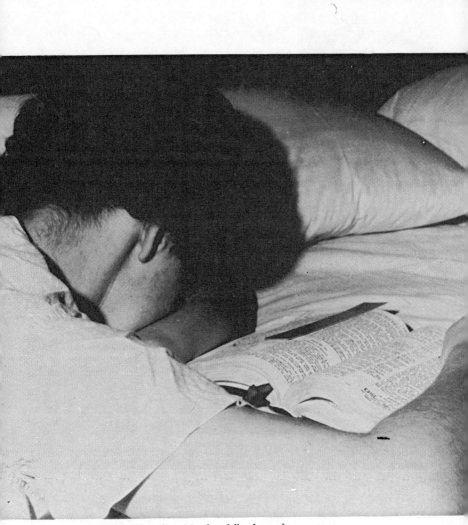

After many an exhausting day, Marilyn fell asleep after her bedside Bible reading and prayers for success of her Wycliffe project.

At long last, after nine years of patient waiting for faster transportation than the dugout canoe, Marilyn got the air service she'd been praying for. The helicopter's coming, for which the villagers had hewn out a landing pad atop her "mountain," was a jungle gala. On a bright day in June 1978, the whole village raced up the hill and joined hands to circle the strip's perimeter, singing and shouting. Honored as the first to fly into the village were Marilyn and her friend Beverly Entz.

Tribespeople did not fully understand the significance of the helicopter, but were thrilled for whatever reason. In a brief speech, Marilyn explained that its chief use would be to transport to hospitals people who were taken with serious sickness or badly hurt in an accident. In such cases, the "flying canoe" (as the people called it) could fly them out of Hauna to a hospital—and all in a matter of minutes, rather than the agonizing hours or days it had taken by river. Having never seen a hospital, been examined by a doctor or flown through the air like a big bird, they comprehended little of all this. But it sounded great, and they cheered the prospect of seeing the 'copter in its lifesaving action.

That chance came soon enough, when a pair of Hauna's men, while felling a big tree for construction of a new church building, had been struck down, breaking their legs. Marilyn's young clinicists forged splints for the broken bones and called for the 'copter, and they were quickly on their way to repairing the damage.

The unfortunate accident had its amusing sidelights. For one thing, while getting the men ready for the trip to the nearest town with a hospital, someone raised the question as to the attire they should wear. The question was apropos, since the older man was garbed in the only haberdashery he ever owned: a thin vine around his waist. Tactfully, Marilyn, who vaguely remembered hearing of a rule that all males going to town were expected to wear pants, at least, cited this to some of the young men. One said, "But, Mama Marilyn, the old one just said that he'd never worn pants in his life and he doesn't expect to start now." The argument went on until the helicopter pilot took a large handkerchief from his pocket, saying, "Here, tuck this into his vine and he'll get by!" That satisfied both tradition and one man's devotion to nonconformity.

However, the two patients had hardly got settled in the hospital when other confusions arose. There was, for example, the matter of the plaster casts. True to tribal habit a tribesman, when going on a journey, however brief, always takes with him his spear, bows and arrows and such travel essentials as his machete. So these two conformed to custom, insisting that these weapons be kept at hand, ready for any emergency.

The hospital staff, however, were somewhat shaken to find that no sooner had the nurses left the room than the pair whacked off the confining plaster casts with their machetes. Calling Hauna on the radio, the pilot said, "Marilyn, the doctors and nurses here are being driven right up the wall by these fellows chopping off their casts with their machetes. Since nobody here speaks their language, we can't get through to them the importance of keeping their casts on. Can't you send us someone who can spell it out for them?" In due time a couple of Sepik Iwams arrived and that issue, too, was solved.

But another problem soon arose to vex the staff. As Marilyn tells it, "The trouble came about from the hospital's policy of allowing the kith and kin of patients—or even just sympathetic fellow New Guineans—to stay with the hospitalized to keep them company. This worked fine in these two cases—until nurses became confused as to who were patients and who were visitors. For the two fellows persisted at first in sleeping *under* the beds while the visitors were happily snoozing *in* the beds. Confusion became confounded when, as a result of the arrangement, it was discovered that nurses were giving shots and pills to the visitors instead of to the patients!"

Despite getting off to such a shaky start with the availability of the helicopter and the hospital care it made possible, the coming of the 'copter did indeed "mark a real breakthrough in the quality of our medical service," as Marilyn put it.

Keeping pace with the growth of literacy and Bible translation was the steady increase in the number of Christian believers and the influence of the little church that Marilyn insisted be centered in the village area.

It was not surprising that growth in the number of Christians was greatest among those who worked on Bible translation under Marilyn's guidance. In seeking the meaning of gospel passages, many found Christ Himself.

It must be admitted, however, that for the majority, conversion from spiritism, ingrained in their culture for untold generations, did not come easily. Nor was Marilyn one to hurry her people into premature acceptance of a faith they had not had time to understand.

"To trust in Christ—really trust—is a long leap for our people," she said. "They naturally ask, 'What will the ancestral spirits do to those who forsake the beliefs of their forefathers? Will the spirits be angry and visit all manner of evils upon us?'"

Most ready to "take the leap," Marilyn found, were the tribe's younger men. Natively intelligent and daring, they had begun to question the tribal ways and were ready to consider a new path to a better life. As a badge of their willingness to identify with Marilyn's God instead of the tribe's ancestral spirits, some of these vigorous young men added to their tribal names such biblical names as Paul, Silas, Joel, Joseph, Gideon, Philip, and John.

But while they were readiest to embrace the new faith, and, eventually, to become the staff leaders of Marilyn's various projects, there were some older men who also dared openly to accept that belief.

Such an early convert was an elderly clan leader and prominent witch doctor, Makabobiya. Almost from the first day of Marilyn's arrival, Makabobiya showed a keen interest in the person and teaching of Jesus. Having long practiced sorcery and other works of the witch doctor, he felt his inner struggle more keenly than did some others. His commitment to Christ came only after months of inquiry into Christian precepts and the development of a willingness to face up to the hard fact that he would have to discontinue his dealings with demons, however costly that step, and put his trust solely in God for deliverance from the powers of darkness. Once taken, he never retraced that step, but became a power for good in the tribe.

Most convincing to other budding Christians in the tribe were three factors: 1) the changed lives such as that of Makabobiya, 2) the vigorous young men who poured their imagination and aid into all of Marilyn's schemes, and 3) the power of prayer. Of the three, prayer (both on the part of Marilyn and her staff and that of her generous supporters back home) was her strongest shield and buckler.

Facing any need that arose, she taught her people to "take it to the Lord in prayer"—and to believe that God not only hears but answers prayer. "Our God is great," she told them again and again, "and He expects us to attempt great things with Him." The result was that again and again the people were witnesses to the answering of her prayers in miraculous ways.

There was, for example, the occasion when, badly needing $800 for a new outboard motor for one of her dugout canoes, she made the need a subject of public prayer. The answer came a few days later in a letter from an Indiana businessman saying, "I've been strangely moved lately by the impression that you have some special need. Please use this gift as you see fit." Enclosed was a check for exactly $800.

And there were times when the people's own prayers were answered in even more spectacular ways. For instance, one of a clan's houses caught fire, threatening to engulf that whole section of the village and reduce it and all its contents to ashes.

The danger of fire and its devastation was nothing new to the people of Hauna. Nor was the dread of it. Their thatched-roof houses, built of the most flammable materials, and huddled close together, were perfect targets for burning. One of the translators described it like this:

"All we translators were busy turning the talk of God into our language, when suddenly we heard shouts of 'Fire! Fire!' People from all parts of the village came running out of their homes, taking up the shout. Our people knew from past experience what fire can do, even when ignited by a single spark. Most of our people still thought of fires as an avenging spirit, visited upon households at some sorcerer's call.

"In a body, we translators raced toward the site from which the smoke and flames were coming. At the scene we saw that a house at the head of a row of houses was aflame. It was impossible to get close enough to be of help in getting out any of the family's possessions. Worse still was the prospect of the holocaust that seemed to be the destiny of the seven other houses in the row. With a strong wind blowing toward them, their destruction appeared inevitable. Already, fingers of flame were reaching out from the burning house toward the next one in the row.

"Standing bunched together facing the flames, our little group of Christians seemed helpless until Joel's strong voice rang out in prayer, above the tumult. 'Oh, Papa God,' he prayed, 'hear my talk. You are the Lord of fire and wind. Only You can keep the flame from consuming these other houses. Put Your arms about those flames and keep them from spreading, Papa God! Show what You can do, so that all the people can see Your strength and power!'

"At that moment the miraculous happened. Suddenly the direction of the wind changed, and the other houses were saved. It was as though Papa God had said to us as He said to the children of Israel facing the sea, 'Stand still and see the salvation of the Lord!'"

The effect of this dramatic prayer's power was electric, for both Hauna's Christians and non-Christians alike. The incident was the subject of wonder for days, leading many to long thoughts about the power and compassion of the Christian's God, as compared to the impotence of the ancestral spirits.

With her literacy classes thriving and her translation workers overflowing all available space, Marilyn saw that she would have to have more facilities or cut back on her program. The latter was unthinkable. This, like her every other need, she saw not as a problem but as an open door and God's voice commanding, "Enter!"

While at home on sick furlough in 1973, she sketched a complete design for the kind of building she would need to house the ever-growing school activities at Hauna. There was nothing small about her plan. Details called for a building 90 feet long by 24 feet wide, and divided into several small rooms and one large room for assembly, well lighted by power supplied by a diesel generator given her by a church at home.

In 1977, Marilyn tackled an even more ambitious building project—an all-purpose community center. Seventy feet long and two stories high, it provided separate rooms for the 14-member translation team, writers' workshops, classes in typing, advanced reading, rudimentary mathematics and recreation. There was also space for Marilyn's living quarters and for visiting tribesmen who, by then, were coming in increasing numbers to view the miracle of Hauna. As she planned it, the structure would tie together all parts of her multiphase program. Included would be a well-stocked store and clinic.

There was, of course, one double-barreled hitch. Where would she find the space for such a building and how would she get permission to build on it? As it was, she was living on sufferance of the chief who owned the "mountain." Could he be persuaded to grant the use of a further part of his land? In other matters Chief Saperi had shown himself friendly enough, but this was a large order.

Back with her tribe after her sick furlough, Marilyn laid her plan before a special meeting of the villagers, then retired to allow the discussion to flow freely. Flow it did—for seven and a half hours.

When the long palaver was over, Saperi himself came to Marilyn's house to report the outcome. She could use whatever portion of land she needed; moreover, his tribesmen would supply native materials and labor. Grinning broadly, Saperi said, "Now is your throat happy, Mama Marilyn?" Offering him the usual cup of coffee, heavily laced with sugar, she said, "Oh, Saperi, I have the happiest throat in all Papua New Guinea!"

When at Ukarumpa, overflowing with joy, she reported on the villagers' acceptance of her ambitious program, some of her WBT/SIL superiors expressed some concern that she just might be getting beyond her financial depth. "It's true we don't have the money for all this," Marilyn replied. "But if the Lord wants it, He will provide." As it turned out, He did.

Actually, the total cost of the project was small. Catching fire from her own enthusiasm, the tribespeople turned the project into an all-village effort. They supplied all the heavy labor—cutting down the huge trees and transporting them by sheer muscle power to the site. The only "outsiders" brought in to help were a couple of skilled carpenters, trained at Ukarumpa, who gave on-the-job training to the village men. They marveled at the villagers' amazing alacrity in learning how to use levels, squares, planes, saws and other tools.

To ward off the rot that assails all native dwellings, Marilyn insisted that the main supports of the big building be of concrete. There being no sand, only muck, in the Hauna area, workers had to take a full day's trip by dugout canoe up the Sepik to find the white sand and stones needed for the making of cement. Unloading from the canoes, the villagers formed a long assembly line, passing the material bucket by bucket from the river to the top of the "mountain."

In the dry season, transporting the huge logs, chosen from the heaviest hardwood, was backbreaking, each requiring 80 men to move and set them in place. Most of the cutting of these immense trees was done in the dry months, then stacked to await floodtime, when they would be loaded on rafts and floated direct to the building site.

Since nails were not commonly available, use was made of heavy rattan vines to fasten struts together. The roof was made from sago palm fronds. Since all these and other materials were in the jungle for the taking, the cost of building materials was almost nil.

During the big building push, Marilyn was here, there and everywhere, keeping track of progress, spurring the people on to greater effort by taking her place in the assembly line and wherever else the work was lagging.

All this outdoor activity, of course, brought Marilyn into constant conflict with her old enemies: ever-present swarms of bugs and mosquitoes, which she hated more than even the crocodiles. To ward off the pests, she and her workers soaked themselves with kerosene and bug repellent. Every few minutes," she reported, "we have to bring out the kerosene jug and spread the stuff over our bodies. We don't smell so good, but it's better than being eaten alive!"

Also, the new construction regularly unearthed her other enemy, snakes. While she adapted herself to other dangers, she never got on friendly terms with these reptiles, many of them 10 feet long or more.

Her worst encounter with a snake occurred one day while she was brushing her teeth in her half-finished house. She felt a movement at her bare feet. Looking down, she saw the head of an enormous reptile, flicking its tongue, eyes staring up at her. "I nearly died on the spot," she says. "But as soon as I moved, the snake disappeared."

As Marilyn had wisely foreseen, the big building project had accomplished something far beyond providing space for her many activities. It had knit together the various clans as nothing else could.

Chapter 15
FIRST CHRISTMAS

Never in the known history of the Sepik Iwam peoples had there been such a blockbuster of a celebration as occurred on Christmas Day, 1977. It was dedication day for the new building. But it was more to Marilyn, much more. To her and some 250 of her people who had become Christians it was not only a highly meaningful observance of the Christ's birth; it was a celebration of the incredible distance the tribe had come during the past few years—out of a stone age into a promising present and glowing future.

The program for the day was not directed by Marilyn but by the people themselves, with Joel, the village pastor, acting as master of ceremonies. After all, she explained, this handsome new building was *their* building, this day *their* day—and God's. So she did not intrude into the festivities except as a worshiper with the people, limiting herself to making quiet suggestions, and then only when asked.

The day before, on Christmas Eve, the whole tribe had fanned out through the jungle to gather wild orchids and other flowers, ferns and colorful leaves to decorate the entire house inside and out. Floral beauty was lavishly spread also over the whole hill, including even the dock, the boats and the motors. The scent of flowers filled the whole village; loud-speakers spread Christmas music and hymns, sung in both the native tongue and in Pidgin. These were mingled with announcements of the day's activities and events.

Since no one was required to attend, it had been anybody's guess how many villagers would attend. But from the first event of the day—a Christian worship service in the church—it was plain that everybody was there. As Joel later reported, "No one's skin was lazy; every villager came. Not one stayed at home."

Next in order of the day's program was a baptismal service for 23 new believers. As with the early worship service, Pastor Joel, assisted by Chief Saperi's appropriate hymns, the new converts entered the Sepik's waters by pairs as two other translators, Silas and Joseph, waited on the banks with towels. Last to be baptized was eighteen-year-old Ann Thomas, short-term helper from the States.

Following the service of baptism, the peal of the village bell summoned the villagers back to the church for the sacrament of Holy Communion. Coconut was served in place of bread, coconut milk in place of wine.

Then came the big event: the dedication of the new house. The villagers were asked to form a ring around the house. Then something seemingly trivial, but of great importance to Marilyn and her work, happened. She had searched in vain for a tribal word for "forgiveness" over the years. Now when the people were asked to join hands, they started to do so. Instead every villager's hand moved to the shoulder of the one next to him.

Marilyn could only give a gasp of delight at the sight of this gesture. As she says, "At this moment we discovered the tribal word for forgiveness—a word for which we translators had long searched."

In the Sepik Iwam culture, when a person puts his arm

around your shoulder, he is asking forgiveness for any wrong he has done you. Tears filled her eyes as the meaning of the gesture swept over her. It was a beautiful act that spoke volumes in testimony to the spiritual growth of her people.

In his dedicatory remarks, Joel reminded the villagers of the long months of toil that had gone into the new building—not forgetting the sacrificial rendering of gifts and prayers by "our American friends" that had made the big project possible. Said Joel, "It has been God, acting through our generous friends, who gave us this beautiful place. And now we give it back to Him."

Coming in for special tribute by Joel and others was the man who, more than anyone else, had brought this dream into reality: the old chief, Saperi. It was he who had given the land for Marilyn's use, and had encouraged her in all her projects.

Sadly, Saperi was not present in the flesh at the dedication. He had died two months before. But during recent years his changed way of life, though unannounced, had been as readily marked as that of any Christian convert in Hauna. That change had been so pronounced that when one speaker at the dedication ceremony regretted his absence, Marilyn's heart cried within her, "But he *is* here. I know it!"

Following the dedication ceremony, the whole village feasted on the foods Marilyn and the people had prepared and distributed. For her part Marilyn had provided great quantities of rice and fish. The villagers had brought sugar cane, crocodile meat, wild pig, sago paste, roasted grubs and other Papua New Guinea delicacies.

The feast over, the villagers hurried to their houses to decorate themselves with painted faces and bodies, flame-colored feathers of jungle birds, multicolored leaves and flowers, then surged forth into a gigantic "singsing." Just as the sun dropped over the horizon, they started joyous dancing and singing which lasted through the night. By morning, with everyone thoroughly exhausted, they trooped off to their houses to sleep.

Never in the recollection of even the oldest tribesman had there ever been so rapturous and historic an occasion among the Sepik Iwams.

Chapter 16

"INCREDIBLE, INCREDIBLE!"

Probably the only person still awake and alert on the day following Hauna's big Christmas celebration was Marilyn herself. Her mind spinning with even bigger dreams for her tribe's future, she sat alone in her new house and let her imagination run. She had a homely motto to explain her devotion to perpetual motion: "You can't steer a boat if it's not moving, and neither can God steer you in any direction if you're not in motion."

One conviction that had nagged at her for months was that ways had to be found to make her village's projects self-supporting. Till now, it had been justifiable to expend every cent of the generous support given her by helpers back home. Justifiable also had been her insistence on paying nominal salaries to her teams of workers who gave full time to teaching and Bible translation, and 40 cents an hour to such part-time workers as the Big Men who spent each evening reviewing the translated work.

But the day would come when she would leave the tribe and they would be on their own, she reminded her adopted people. If the village was to continue going forward, it had to have a sound economic as well as spiritual base.

Money-earning projects, geared to their needs and lifestyle, that would make them self-sufficient, were required to carry on learning and development. The trouble with the people having money, however, was that there was not a single place within 100 miles to spend it.

Marilyn's first answer to that problem was the setting up of a small store at Hauna, bringing in from Ambunti and Ukarumpa a small stock of things that appealed to them. Now, with the new building, she enlarged the store, appointed a committee of three to manage it and taught them the rudiments of accounting. All projects were to be turned into support of the school.

The Hauna store's immediate success stimulated in Marilyn's mind a bright idea: Why not a *floating* store—one that could take salable goods of one kind and another to other tribes along the Sepik, with the extra duties of spreading the Gospel and treating the sick? Growing increasingly excited at the thought of her "gospel ship," the dream craft began taking on the dimensions of a houseboat, large enough to carry a generous supply of trade items and medicines, plus provision and sleeping space for its crew of four when staying overnight, plus deck room for evangelistic meetings and Bible teaching.

To test her dream's practicality, Marilyn loaded two of her largest motor-propelled canoes with a stock of practical items such as axes, shovels, clothing from her "missionary barrel," fishing nets, hooks and lines, native food items. She then recruited a quartet of Hauna's most dependable young men, and sent them out on the watery safari. The men were back in less than a week with more than $1,000 in gross earnings. A second voyage two weeks later produced an even larger profit.

Persuaded that her income-producing scheme was feasible, Marilyn began looking around for used boats suitable to her purpose. Her high hopes drooped a bit when she found that the right kind of craft had a price tag of $30,000. But her hopes rapidly rebounded when, mentioning her dream, she quickly received pledges for $25,000.

As one observer put it, "Having seen Marilyn's faith work miracles in other matters, even the most careless player of odds would be ill-advised to wager against her dream ship coming in—when, as she put it, 'God wants us to have it.'"

While she awaited God's clear word, the floating stores operating from canoes went on spreading the gospel and selling goods. In no time at all these were providing enough income to pay the salaries not only of the schoolteachers and translators but of all 83 paid workers on Marilyn's staff.

To sound out official reaction to her determination to make her Hauna projects self-supporting, Marilyn coaxed a high official of the Papua New Guinea government to visit Hauna. She took him through the new building, showing him the school filled with eager youngsters learning to read and write their own language, the well-stocked clinic with a long line of patients being served, the fleet of canoes and docks, and shared with him her plans to make the whole enterprise self-supporting.

"In a few years I'll be leaving all this in the hands of these beautiful people," she told him. "I'll probably go out from the Sepik with nothing but my toothbrush."

As he trooped over Marilyn's mountain, the man from Wewak muttered, "Incredible! Incredible!"

It isn't known whether, in using that descriptive, the official from Wewak was referring to his hostess or to the innovative moves by which she was so successfully shepherding the Sepik Iwams out of the darkness into the light. Most likely it was to both.

Chapter 17
STRANGE HAPPENINGS AT HAUNA

Well aware of the Holy Spirit's working in those He calls, Marilyn knew that the Christians at Hauna would, sooner or later, be confronted with the missionary mandate to "go into all the world and preach the Gospel to every living creature."

In discussions with the people—especially the tribe's growing body of Christians—she often stressed that the Christian faith was not a jewel to be jealously owned and guarded by a chosen few; it had to be shared. Any effort to keep it to themselves would only diminish it. Not shared, it would die.

But "into the whole world"? That was hard for them to grasp. From pictures clipped from magazines, maps that she'd spread out before them and projected color slides, she had imparted to them some idea of the world's vastness and the many kinds, colors and lifestyles of its peoples. But all these were so far away. How could they, a tiny tribe in a place that was but a small dot on the map, have any effect in that big, wide world?

Marilyn turned their attention from the global to the particular. Patiently she explained, "Think of the part of the world you can touch and see. That includes your tribe, your family, the neighbor who lives next to you. It includes even your enemies. That's your world, the only one you are responsible for."

It was while the Sepik Iwams were mulling over this strange doctrine that their neighboring world began coming to them. From all up and down the Sepik, from dozens of little villages and tributaries within their reach, the jungle grapevine began circulating news of the strange happenings at Hauna. Tales spread of a young white woman living with the Sepik Iwams, speaking their language, showing them how to carve their talk on a banana leaf, of new buildings going up, of motor-driven canoes going up and down the river on mysterious errands.

And they were puzzled. What did it all mean? Were the Hauna warriors planning some kind of raid on their neighbors? To get some answers, curious visitors from near and far—some of them former enemies—paddled their canoes past Hauna, straining to get a glimpse inside the settlement.

First of the visitors bold enough to call were members of the four other tribes making up the Sepik Iwam language group. These came not on their own but at the invitation of the Hauna Christians whom Marilyn had persuaded to demonstrate their missionary impulses. A canoe sent from Hauna to invite a couple of their people for a look-see came back with not two but eight men. The Hauna people made them welcome, provided them with food and sleeping space, and proudly showed off their school, church, clinic, village store and other facilities. Then, as the *piece de resistance*, they displayed their ability to read and write their own *ples tok* (native language).

Upon their return to their tribal villages, the visitors, with their exciting tales, sparked a native rush to Hauna. The result? Marilyn and her staff soon found that her parish population had leaped to some 1,600 people, instead of the usual 400. All were pleading for teachers and schools of their own. However, the spread of literacy fever was not limited to the Sepik Iwam group. Delegations from tribes farther afield began showing up.

One such was a canoe-load of people who had made a four-day journey to verify reports of the "white missis" who worshiped a living God who, unlike their ancestral spirits, brought His followers only good.

This crop of guests bowed before the "white missis" that people called Mama Marilyn. Spokesman for the group was a short black man who spoke Pidgin and whose special interest seemed centered on Hauna's village church. Taking him and others through the little church, Marilyn said, "The God we follow is everywhere. This is His house. Here we come to meet Him, sing His praises and seek His guidance. It is His talk that we are carving on the banana leaf."

When the spokesman relayed this to the group, a loud babble ensued, and then he turned to Marilyn: "My people want to know if you will come to our village and carve God's talk for us!"

"Carving any talk on the banana leaf takes a long time," explained Marilyn. "I have only a few more years before I finish my work here with the Sepik Iwam tribe. But we will pray that the Holy Spirit will help us find someone to go to your village to give God's talk to your people."

The spokesman wanted something more definite. "But cannot you just come to visit our village?" he persevered. She promised to try.

For days Marilyn couldn't get the man's plaintive insistence out of her mind. Finally, with a companion, she set out, traveling all day by motor canoe, wading through swamps and climbing over mountains, until at last they arrived in the village. Who should come bounding out to meet them but their Pidgin-speaking friend!

"Mama Marilyn," he shouted, "you did not forget!" Delight was in his face, tears in his eyes. "You kept your promise!"

As they talked, Marilyn caught sight of a bright new structure in the village center. "What is that building?" she asked.

With pride glistening in his eyes, he replied, "Oh, that's our church!"

Mystified, she said, "But I don't understand. Has a missionary come here? Or do you have a pastor?"

Brightly he replied, "Oh, no, Mama Marilyn, we have seen nobody."

"But why have you built that beautiful little church?"

He replied, "You told us that the Holy Spirit would find us someone to give us God's carving. We want to be ready."

Still she persisted. "But if someone doesn't come soon, what then?"

His answer was in two words only. But packed in those two words was a shining faith that down the ages has been the glorious "substance of things hoped for, the evidence of things not seen."

He said, *"We wait."*

Chapter 18
HOW MANY OR HOW MUCH?

Gidion

Philip

One unique aspect of Wycliffe Bible Translators' policy is its willingness to concentrate the work of some of its ablest people on the smallest tribes—some of them with no more than a few hundred members. That policy has no better exemplar than Marilyn Laszlo—and no champion more convinced of its reasonableness.

Often the policy is challenged whenever and wherever she presents the Wycliffe story to audiences at home and abroad. "With so many larger tribes needing the Word, isn't it a waste of time, talent and effort to ask your people to spend 15 or more years—the best of their lives—on such insignificant clusters of people?"

If the word "insignificant" is used, Marilyn's hackles tend to rise. Then calming, she is likely to reply, "If our Lord intends, as He declared, to make up His 'bride' from every tribe and tongue, how dare we call these small tribes insignificant? And how about Christ's words to the Pharisees: 'What man among you, having a hundred sheep, if he loses one of them, doth not leave the ninety and nine in the wilderness and go after that which is lost, until he finds it?' And if we neglect the one while saving the ninety-nine, what excuse can we offer our Lord to whom the one is always as important as the many?"

While WBT is at work among many large tribes, some ranging up to as many as 100,000 members, the small tribes are not forgotten. It is this policy that attracts the praise of the thoughtful public. As *Time* magazine commented in a recent issue, "Most Bible societies concentrate mainly on getting adequate translations into the major written languages. But the Summer Institute of Linguistics has a longer reach. For the past 42 years, following the teachings of its founder, W. Cameron Townsend, SIL teams have been seeking out tiny, isolated tribes in remote corners of the world."

With her "longer reach" presently embracing the 1,600 members of the Sepik Iwam language group—with special emphasis on the 400 or so members comprising the four Hauna clans—Marilyn's tribe fits into *Time's* category.

In a meeting where Marilyn spoke of her work, the pastor of a homeland church commented, "I just don't see giving your whole life to such a small group."

Marilyn countered, "I'm sure you haven't thought that through, sir. Certainly you and I both know a number of pastors who are giving their entire lives to congregations of fewer than 500 people—some, even fewer than 100. Does that mean that these faithful ministers are wasting their time and talents? I'm sure that the God who called them to their humble ministry does not think so—nor do those 'called ones' themselves."

Pausing for an instant, Marilyn added, "I have been serving and living among the Sepik Iwam tribe for eight years, and during that time we have seen well over 400 people come to know the Lord Jesus Christ. Tell me, am I really wasting my time and talents when God has so honored our efforts?"

To others she has often said, "Let no one call drudgery this kind of ministry. The important thing is not how many or how few we are working among; rather, it is how faithful we are in performing the work God has called us to, and how firmly we stay in the center of His will for us. "

In pursuing that objective, Marilyn has found a life she describes as "exciting and adventurous—a very richly rewarding experience, to say the least."

Chapter 19
SUMMING UP

While Marilyn never entertained nagging doubts about her manifold labors, there was one question that did obtrude on rare occasions. Such an occasion followed the big Christmas celebration in 1977. With the old year fast fading and the new year coming on, she had had moments of introspection, letting her mind rove over the testing and triumphs of her years in the tribe. And suddenly an uninvited question arose: *Had it all been worthwhile?*

Such shadowy doubts never came during the usual flurry of work with the tribe—only when she was bone-tired from the unremitting task of coping with health and medical problems, her own and the tribe's . . . from the long journeys by dugout canoe . . . from the constant trips back and forth to Ambunti for supplies . . . from the frequent runs by canoe and air to and from the Ukarumpa base to check and recheck her own growing knowledge of the tribal language, and to go over and over again with WBT's expert consultants the Bible translations she and her team worked out . . . from the long strivings to give clarity and meaning to the Scriptures . . . from the endless typing and retyping and proofreading . . . from the never-ending production of primers and story books to keep up with the students' advance in knowledge.

Like the Apostle Paul, she has experienced more than her share of "journeyings often, of perils of waters, perils in the wilderness, of weariness and painfulness." And all this had taken its toll.

Then, even when home on furlough for rest and recuperation, there were the constant rounds of deputation tours to keep her supporters informed and to raise needed funds to initiate her new projects. And there is the loneliness of those times when she had to carry the full burden of her program, relieved only by needed companionship from short-term helpers who could be recruited to come out to the tribe.

At such times she would experience a fleeting thought: *Is it all worthwhile?* And, as always, there would come an inner voice she felt was God's: "Marilyn, I understand your weariness and your loneliness. But look at Joel, and at Dani, Joseph, James and all the others—and especially at the hundreds of Sepik Iwams who have been turned from the evil spirits to become My followers. Are they not worth it all?" And the inner voice would seem to continue, "And look to your mountain, Marilyn, and see how, though once a place of darkness and despair, we together have turned it into a mountain of light. Have I not promised that the people who sit in darkness would see a great light, and for those who dwell in the region and shadow of death, a great light would dawn?"

Dropping to her knees, Marilyn would reply from her heart, "Yes, Lord, oh yes, they are worth it and more!"

Nights without number were given to such bedside communion with her Master. Such "little talks with God" were not for herself alone but for all those forgotten tribespeople of more than 2,000 tongues, and for all those dedicated ones who would find challenge and fulfillment in taking the Gospel to them in their own languages.

And always God's voice would seem to say, "And, Marilyn, how about all those faithful ones back home whose prayers and gifts have supported you through the years? Are they not worth keeping faith with?"

Then, rising from her knees refreshed, she could joyfully plunge once again into the task to which God had called her from early childhood, her heart singing with the song that has become a sort of WBT/SIL international anthem:

"Faith, mighty faith, the promise sees
And looks to God alone;
It laughs at impossibilities,
And cries, 'It shall be done!'"

ACKNOWLEDGEMENTS

It would have been impossible to write this book without the guidance and help of many people within and without the Wycliffe family.

The author's deepest appreciation goes, of course, to Marilyn Laszlo, who so generously made herself available to answer what must have seemed endless questions probing into her life and work.

Grateful acknowledgement must also be given to "Uncle Cam" and his wife Elaine for freely opening their files and memories to supply interesting sidelights on Marilyn's hopes and dreams, and to Dr. Bruce Hooley, director of SIL/WBT's Papua New Guinea base, for his careful checking of the manuscript for possible errors of fact.

Of all those who shared information and photographs depicting Marilyn's work on the Sepik River, two are deserving of special mention. One is Mrs. Beverly Entz, whose assistance during long months of assembling material was invaluable. The wife of a WBT aviation expert now stationed at JAARS headquarters in Waxhaw, North Carolina, Beverly knew Marilyn in New Guinea and joined with her in a duo that has traveled widely and earned plaudits wherever they have sung together.

The second person eminently worthy of being singled out for an expression of appreciation is Sanna Barlow Rossi of Bradenton, Florida. No stranger to New Guinea, Mrs. Rossi in 1952 and 1953 traveled extensively across this forgotten land under the aegis of Gospel Recordings, Inc. Inspired by "Uncle Cam" Townsend and his Wycliffe translators, she and her husband, Anthony Rossi, became among WBT's most generous and consistent supporters.

Mrs. Rossi is author of *God's City in the Jungle*, a deeply inspiring book describing WBT's work among the Ticuna tribe in Peru.

To all these and scores more, the author is deeply indebted.